COUNSELING WITH SINGLE ADULTS

Counseling with SINGLE ADULTS

NANCY D. POTTS

BROADMAN PRESS
Nashville, Tennessee

4232–25

ISBN: 0–8054–3225 6

Dewey Decimal Classification: 301.43

Subject heading: SINGLE ADULTS

Library of Congress Catalog Card Number: 77–91690
Printed in the United States of America

TO

**The Single Adults of
South Main Baptist Church**

They've been a part of my journey and
have permitted me to be a part of some of theirs.
Their willingness to take the risk
of being real has helped me learn
that which cannot be taught.

**Thank you for sharing some of life's
most important lessons.**

Acknowledgments

I wish to express my appreciation and friendship for the following people.

. . . To Ken Chafin—for catching the vision of a singles ministry and for being willing to share what you learn on your journey.

. . . To Dan Yeary—for building a solid foundation that is now being built upon and for my beginning.

. . . To Dick Stafford—for your sensitivity and ability to minister to individuals and for a relationship in which I trust enough to be what I feel.

. . . To Marilyn Hamor—for your perseverance through endless days of typing and rewrites and for hearing ideas before I've been comfortable enough to write them.

Contents

Considerations for the Counselor

Preface

Words can kill or bring life depending on how we use them. For that reason writing is an intensely painful process for me. Transferring thoughts onto paper demands that I search my awareness, my experiences, and my solitude. People ask, "How's it going?" and I reply, "It's going . . . sometimes forward, sometimes in reverse, but it's going." When I get stuck and wonder if I'll ever have another creative moment, I momentarily think about quitting. Friends ask if they can be helpful, and their caring helps. But writing is a solitary, not a group, experience. I reenter the life of the book and begin again.

And so it is with life. Endings and beginnings, and sometimes being stuck in the dirty middle! Life is full of paradoxes . . . I'm convinced that the more I learn, the less I know. My simplistic solutions for life's problems were given up about the time I asked myself, *Do you want to look good or do you want to learn something?* I opted to learn, for we get no more than we're willing to risk.

Knowing that much background about me, you may understand my trepidation when I was asked to write this book. The audience, said the publishers, would be those who work with single adults. That meant ministers, laymen, educators, and singles themselves. Each has a different frame of reference and understanding of what counseling means.

For instance, ministers in training learn to "be good" and "have answers" to life's questions. Yet an overemphasis on being good makes it difficult to grant self-acceptance. And without self-acceptance there's a tendency to deny evil in oneself. The net result is an attempt to rescue others from their problems.

As a marriage and family therapist, my role is to help others accept their imperfect, finite conditions so that they can become more of who they are. It's also to work within the context of family relationships and facilitate the system's change toward greater health. That requires unhooking the scapegoat and viewing what occurs in the room as real, not as good or bad. Labels become our tombstones. Whether trained in pastoral care, education, social work, or psychology, each counselor teaches the rules of his own group. So each of us must unlearn some of what we've learned if we're to respond in a growth relationship. But our role doesn't end there. We will have to be willing to learn that which cannot be easily taught.

It's naive to believe that if we tell people what areas we think they need help with or improvement in, we give them the ability to help themselves. We are neither that powerful nor that insightful! We don't know another person's story; we will have to discover it. But it's nice to know that really "hard travelin' " doesn't have to be done alone.

This book is an introduction to experiencing more of who you can be, to people who are single, to some of the struggles that accent life. What goes into the struggle to be a whole person is mentioned; how you respond, and at what point, is up to you. The chapters are designed to offer practical aids. However, each chapter could be expanded into a book. So you'll discover that they touch on the subject, but you'll have to complete the experience for yourself. Of all the aids suggested, none is *the* way to respond; rather, each is one place to begin. Find out what works for you.

I have not burdened the book with theological and psychological jargon. Although I view the two concepts as being integrated into one, labels and Scriptures can be a way to maintain distance. Often we quote the Scriptures to avoid dealing with how we feel about someone or something. Or we label a person so that we don't have to get to know him as he is. You can read the book from your own theological frame of reference. Take what fits; question what doesn't.

In recognition of the *he/she* problem that sometimes exists, the editors and I have agreed to use *he.* So in some cases you'll read *he* referring to a person in general. Ladies, don't feel neglected; that decision was made for simplicity's sake.

Before you go any further, you might want to understand my bias about singles. Those at South Main Baptist Church and in other parts of the country have taught me much. As they've risked telling me their stories, I've come to appreciate and respect them. Some of the singles I've met are creative, bright, and growth-oriented individuals. Many face the pain of divorce or death of a spouse and choose to grow through the experience. Others are using singleness as an opportunity to accept their wholeness. They're beginning to live their todays rather than dwelling on the past or future. Single is a viable life-style option. But let us not make singlehood or marriage an image of perfection. Each of us has one lifetime—we can live it or tolerate a living death. The choice is ours!

NANCY POTTS

1 When the Familiar Becomes the Problem

I have never begun a first interview in which what is presented as the problem really was the issue. Within the confusion of some crisis, a person comes for counseling. It's a personal quest in which a person searches for he's not sure what. Depending on the language of the client, it may be peace, love, hope, God, freedom, or curiosity about what the future will hold.

Usually, it's not a dedication to growth that brings a person to my office. Rather, it's fear. For some reason, the tried and true ways of relating are not paying off. So there's distress, pain, and disruption in the everyday routine of life. Singles don't have a corner on that market; that's true with most of us. We tend to rest with the familiar until the familiar becomes the problem. We live with our behavior for as long as it works. We stay with secure misery because change is threatening and unfamiliar.

So a client comes hoping that I can tell him how to be happy without changing. He wants an answer to the unspoken question "What is unchanging and dependable in my life?" Of course, I have no such wisdom. The task of each individual is to learn to be responsible for his life, however much of a mixed bag it is!

So, whether a person is dealing with loneliness, intimacy,

sexuality, divorce, marriage, or death, he's looking for meaning. Often he hopes that I will be a parent figure who will share the secret for finding that happily-ever-after time in which there's no pain.

If you're going to work with people and their struggles, you'll have to move from thinking you have all of the answers to simply offering a place to wrestle with all that a person doesn't understand. You'll have to avoid giving dogma and give yourself instead. You'll have to give up the role of teacher and become a learner. You'll have to preach fewer sermons and find meaning in the questions. You'll have to stop giving someone what you think he needs to know and instead help him to discover that which he already possesses. Instead of encouraging dependence on your "wisdom," you will aid the struggler in learning from his own journey and then leaving you.

Sometimes that means allowing a person to make mistakes in order to grow from them. It means resisting the temptation to become more than you are. It means listening to another relate his story so that he can release himself from his past. It's recognizing that each of us has the choice of making our past a prison or a gate to further growth. It means being vulnerable to another's pain, but not becoming responsible for it. It requires that you be willing to confront the darker side of yourself—the thoughts and feelings and ideas that you've labeled good or bad, strong or weak, and right or wrong.

It means taking a chance and rising to the needs of the moment as one who cares. You'll have to view life as problem-solving. If you slip into thinking that there is a magic happily-ever-after time in your own life, you change your own role as fellow struggler to that of answer giver. It is above all realizing that you too are imperfect, and there will be times when you "blow it" in your own life.

Ministering or counseling or being a friend to single adults is simply being who you are with another person. This book is concerned with singles because it's time to take seriously the individuals in this group. And because crisis is often the initiator into singlehood, within this group you may find many who are on journeys of personal growth. For whatever reason, status quo has changed. So the personal quest for wholeness, meaning, and creativity has begun.

If we don't become too sophisticated, too analytical, too dogmatic, or too cynical, we can be open to the patterns of our lives and their lessons. Most of us say that we're too burdened by our own experiences to be curious and empathetic to others' struggles. In truth, we're just too helpless, blind, and naive. We lack understanding of our technical world and our own place and time and response in it. Our bewilderment with our own emotions and reactions causes us to look at others with uncomprehending eyes. We lose our curiosity about how others see themselves, their world, and their relationships, not because we know too much, but because we'd have to confront ourselves in the process.

Being available to another person's growth means that you begin with principles that relate to yourself. Sometimes it means that you give up the arrogant assumption that something "important," as defined by you, happens in each meeting. It may be that being present to another is in itself important. It may mean that your time together and whatever occurs is not labeled good or bad, but real. It may mean that now, today in your hectic schedule, you choose time to examine your own expectations for being related in a counseling or ministering process to single adults.

Before you can understand the struggles of someone else, you must begin your own process of self-discovery. For instance:

1. Have you been single yourself? How did you relate to your single status? How did you feel about yourself during that time?

If you've had a period of singlehood, you have a frame of reference for understanding some of the unique challenges of that period. However, that's only a partial understanding. Your age, set of circumstances, and goals were unique to you. Consequently, you don't want your history to prevent you from being curious about how life is for someone else. Two people often experience the same event differently!

If you moved from your family of origin directly into marriage, you didn't have the opportunity to "make it on your own" as a single. But you can't assume that your life-style is one everyone wants, regardless of how content or discontent you might be.

Whatever your personal history, the significant factor in forming relationships with singles or anyone else is the ability to understand and accept how each person experiences his or her own world.

2. How do you feel about singles? What are your preconceived definitions of people who are single?

How you stereotype a group influences how you view the individuals who are members of it. If you've never had a personal relationship with someone who is single, where have you formed your image of singleness? The media? Books? Movies? Relatives? People who have never married, who have divorced, and who are widowed have their own identities, self-concepts, and degrees of self-esteem. So throw out your generalizations. If you attempt to pigeonhole people, you'll miss the chance to know individuals in all their realness, creativity, and uniqueness. Pigeonholes are havens for pigeons, not people.

3.   How do you understand the dynamics that occur in divorce, widowhood, and remarriage? Do you have more than a textbook perception?

Stereotypes are in abundance, but seldom fit. Not every single person wants to be married. Not every divorced woman is sexually available. Divorced men do hurt. Not all widows and widowers give up living after the death of their mates. Check out your personal stereotypes; keeping them will affect how you relate. It's difficult to see someone as real if a wall of stereotypes separates you!

4.   What are your expectations for the relationship with a single adult? What role do you expect to play in the relationship?

Do you have an agenda for what you think is best for someone? Do you give advice as input for someone to make a decision? Do you become angry if your advice isn't taken? In other words, do you become a parent figure who robs a person of the responsibility to guide his life? Part of adulthood is learning to make decisions and accepting whatever consequences go with them. If you become a parent figure or a rescuer, you don't do anyone a favor. Fostering dependency only provokes anger and disappointment on both sides. Examine your own needs in light of how you relate to singles. It takes two to set up a dependency relationship.

5.   How do you view your role as a catalyst?

If a person tries to manipulate you into telling him how to be happy or successful, he's asking you to be responsible for his life. You could be seduced into playing an impossible, godlike role. If you can listen without cluttering the air with simplistic solutions (after all, if there were an easy answer, it would already have been discovered!) or ritualistic advice, then you've taken the first step. You're offering someone the privilege of telling his story while you seek to interpret and to provide emotional acceptance and support. It takes courage to say, "I don't understand; I don't have all the answers." You can't hide behind walls of doctrine if you're offering someone the invitation to share how he *really feels.* You've crossed a pivotal bridge if you can provide such an atmosphere—the bridge that recognizes that all feelings are acceptable and that each of us is responsible for our choices and their consequences.

6.   What do you do with your feelings of disappointment and anger? Is counseling others a way you deal with unresolved anger or disappointment that has occurred in your own family?

Spend time in reflection over your own life experiences. Think back to the last time you felt disappointed. Perhaps you didn't achieve a goal; a relationship died; a meeting turned out badly; or you felt unacceptable. What did you do with your feelings of disappointment? Think. Did you suppress them, become depressed, withdraw, cry, get angry, or talk about them with the person involved? Only by first dealing with disappointment are we free to enjoy the good things about an experience.

At the end of a weekend seminar I once attended, the leader asked us to rate the value of the three days. He drew a horizontal line across the wall and placed a 1 at one end and a 10 at the opposite end. We were requested to stand beside the number representing the degree to which our expectations for the retreat had been met. Slowly, everyone moved toward a number. After everyone had placed themselves, we noticed that the majority of people were in front of the 6, 7, or 8. The leader then remarked that dealing with the disappointments freed us to take the useful part of the weekend with us. The point is that disappointment blocks growth unless we both acknowledge and deal with it.

Closely connected with disappointment is anger. We all get angry, but how we deal with it is another matter. Some of us grew up believing there were good and bad emotions. Unfortunately, anger was tossed into the "Christians don't" column! Emotions are healthy, and anger is our release valve to deal with crisis situations. It's not the feelings that cause us problems; it's how we deal with them. What do you do with your anger—pretend it isn't there; verbally snipe at people; turn anger in on yourself and get depressed; blame other people?

Learning to claim anger, face the feelings, and appropriately deal with them is a process that requires practice. If you see anger as bad, you'll verbally or nonverbally encourage others to suppress their feelings while in your presence. If you're talking with someone going through a divorce or the death of a mate, anger is a necessary part of the grief work. If you can hear a person without communicating that "you shouldn't feel that way," you may help him or her toward a healthy readjustment.

As you may realize, how you deal with your own emotions and feelings plays a large part in how you permit others to deal with theirs in your presence.

7.   What can you offer to persons seeking your help?

You can't take someone further than you've been yourself. In fact, sometimes the help needed is to point out the paths *not* to take when someone is at the crossroads. That requires that you have some understanding of the dangers as well as the promises of each path. How else could you respond appropriately to another's dilemma? You too must have at some time known the fear, the apprehension, the excitement of being tugged in various directions.

This book is not intended to be a substitute for personal counseling, for you can't have a dynamic relationship with printed pages. It's not the answer to some hidden agenda, for the book is intended to provoke questions. It's not a way to sidestep your own journey, but an encouragement to continue. Hopefully the book will offer "handles," a way to understand and relate to some of the significant hurdles that face single adults.

Comments of singles actively facing life will give you a clue to the stories represented on these pages:

"As John's coffin was lowered I thought, *How can I go on? They're burying me too.*"

"Why did it happen to me? I've tried to live a good life!"

"But no one prepared me for divorce. It's as though part of me died, while part of me is uncontrollably angry."

"If someone asks one more time, 'Why isn't a nice girl like you married?' I may throw up."

"The loneliness is whipping me into a living death."

"How can I be sure another marriage will work? I feel so vulnerable and afraid. I can't risk another failure."

"My sexual needs are overwhelming. The 'cold shower' routine is a worn-out cliché that no one follows. Right?"

"How can I tell if a relationship is healthy or unhealthy? And how do you say good-bye?"

"I'm afraid to trust."

"I'm single by choice. I wish people wouldn't look at me as though I'm strange."

"I'm thirty-five and my mother treats me like a seventeen-year-old."

"God, help me. Being a single parent demands more energy than I can muster."

"Is it ever too late to learn to like yourself?"

"The tears are scalding. When will the pain end?"

"Just because I'm not married doesn't mean I'm frigid."

"Loneliness is like a raw nerve."

"What does it mean to be a Christian single?"

"Who can I turn to?"

"The hardest thing about being divorced is that some men think I'm sexually starved and available."

"Single, ready or not."

Singles are a diverse group. Some deal with the trauma of divorce; others are widowed but remain "married to their dead mates"; still others are unmarried but feel pressure from a coupled world. However, there's another group of singles who aren't striving for marriage. Instead, their priority is to live creative lives as singles. Single is a viable lifestyle option! It's OK to be single! But regardless of how a single adult sees himself or his growth, there are still very real practical problems—how to deal with society's negative attitudes, to get a good seat in a restaurant, to deal with credit, insurance, or loan discrimination. Even hearing sermons on families with no mention of single-parent families can pose its own problems!

When people are unsettled by crisis, doubt, or anxiety, they have the best opportunity for personal growth. Feelings of uneasiness prompt us to find a counselor, clergyman, friend, or someone we view as a leader. That person may be you.

Every time a person meets you, he already has an image of what you're like. The visual picture could be completely drawn in with colors, expressions, and fantasies about your reactions. Or it may be a picture borrowed from someone else. That someone is whoever told him about you and how you perform in relationships.

Naturally, how you view yourself is seldom how someone else pictures you. Hence, it's advisable to ask the person to introduce his visual picture to you. The first few minutes of an interview is the time to understand a person's expectations of you, as well as gain vital information about the problem.

It's useful to begin by inquiring about the person's feelings about coming to see you. Reactions might range among scared, shy, looking forward to it, guilty, ready, and so forth. It takes courage to think about telling someone about yourself. If you're a minister, there may be feelings of shame or fears of rejection. Or perhaps you're a father figure, and the person unrealistically hopes that you can make everything OK. He might wonder if you can be trusted not to tell the church staff about his problems in the name of concern or prayer or anxiety. Or perhaps he's concerned that his story will be the next anecdote in your sermon! If you're not a minister but work with singles as a director, friend, or teacher, the issues are similar. Each person to some degree has feelings about confiding in you and concern over what you'll do with the information. Confidentiality may not be expressed as an open request, but rest assured that it is an issue.

Another piece of the puzzle is in regard to who referred the person to you. Was it someone you helped once before, so the expectation is that you'll do it again? Was it another minister? What is the relationship between the client and the referral source and, for that matter, between you and the referral source? Being curious about how the referral was made and what was said about you will give you an idea about any unspoken expectations.

Naturally, you'll want to get some feel for what the client labels as the problem and how he views it. Why is it that *now* the problem seems unmanageable? How has it been handled in the past? What does the person want to change? Again, you're not trying to solve anything; you're attempting to understand what all this means to the client. I remember one single adult who wanted to discuss "educational change." However, questions revealed that the man was dealing with sexual identity issues. The job change was merely a smoke screen; he was unhappy in his job, but that wasn't causing the intense pain and grief.

On the other hand, a woman talked freely of her sexual involvements twenty minutes into the interview. She was more comfortable talking about her sex acts than discovering that she was afraid of men. Again, what is presented as the problem may be an aspect of the discomfort. But people generally deal with their anxiety in a new relationship by talking about what is least threatening. For one person, the theme may be surface conservation; for another it may be fears, sexuality, or careers. That's why it's imperative that you hear what's being said on two levels. The first level is what is being labeled as the problem; and the second is revealed when the theme of those first few minutes has been discussed enough that the client can begin to tell you about the real issue.

Part of your ability to help may come in helping the client look at the problem from a different perspective. Each of us has a mind-set about how we view problems and deal with them. But sometimes that in itself is part of the problem.

Again, you're not rushing in to fix something. You're trying to understand what's happening from the single adult's perspective! That includes discovering the answer to the question: "Who am I to you, and how can I be helpful?" The client may look at you curiously as if you're supposed to know the answers to that. But don't let your anxiety throw you off-balance. The unspoken expectation may be for you to bury a relationship, save a marriage, absolve guilt, allow him to dump emotions on you, provide an easy answer, play funeral director for a marriage, have an affair, and so forth. It's your responsibility to decide what you can and cannot do, how you will work with a client, and on what time schedule. The two of you may have to talk at length about an acceptable contract—that is, what you can realistically offer. Unkept promises only create anger, emotional distance, and a rationalization for not working through problems.

In some instances, your best response may be one in which you refer a person for professional counseling. If you're a minister who is trained in counseling and you have the time and interest, your decision may be to see the person yourself. However, either way, it's vital that you make the decision in the client's best interest. Being manipulated by pleas, emotions, or anger will sabotage the whole process.

If you're a friend, you might be most helpful by permitting the person to talk about whatever fears are associated with seeking professional help. You want to take care not to permit someone to use your concern as a dumping ground for unresolved issues. In those cases, talking lets the steam out of the steam kettle, but it always builds up again! Sometimes you can be a better friend by encouraging someone to seek counseling, while you continue the friendship as part of the support system.

Just as you take the first step of awareness in asking "Who am I?" you take a step along the path of wisdom in acknowledging your limitations. You're then free to respond to another's pain without guiding someone into your unknown.

Considerations for Times Alone

2 How Come You're Not Married?

Carol labored long and hard to overcome her self-dissatisfaction with being unmarried. She entered counseling with congested feelings of pity, rage, and disappointment. Her description of herself was that of a victim. She blamed her parents, friends, God, and herself for being thirty-six and single. For years she'd been secretly spiteful of those who were married, whether happily so or not.

Her quest for identity as a woman meant that she had to give up her role as victim. She'd worn it as a badge and used its power to avoid dealing with her own insecurities. After all, blaming others is a useful way to abdicate taking responsibility for your life! Carol had much to learn, and a greater amount to unlearn, in her pilgrimage to take care of herself.

First, she had to learn to face her stubborn desire to be taken care of by daddy, husband, or some other male figurehead. It's a long struggle from experiencing oneself as a powerless nonperson to someone of worth and wholeness. Carol equated marriage with what the church, society, parents, and friends expected of her. So she saved time, plans, and emotions for the day she'd marry. It never occurred to her that she had a choice about marriage. Nor did the fact that she lived on the edge of panic motivate her to develop her personal interests and goals. She postponed living and sacrificed living the present on the altar of others' expectations.

Now she sifted through her tears as she grieved over a relationship that had just ended. Carol and Don had dated for only three months, but she'd tried to manipulate the relationship into permanence. In emptiness and loneliness, she voiced the irony—she had feared Don would pull back, and he had.

Over the course of counseling, Carol began to discover something real in herself. She did have choices. And slowly she came to value her own thoughts and wishes. She began to evaluate her life—where she was going, her present career, and so forth. No longer did she diminish herself and perceive herself as a second-class woman. Carol had begun to lift herself out of the fog of worthlessness and inadequacy. Her pain would continue to be crucial in helping her to love herself. No longer the victim, she was choosing to take charge of her life.

Carol's tale reflects the panic that many feel at the prospect of living single. Life becomes a postponement, so lost is the opportunity to use singleness as a time of growth. What makes it even more difficult is that each of us walks the tightrope of paradox—we must learn to live today as though it's all the time we have, while at the same time planning for tomorrow.

Singleness can be a productive, creative life-style if it's viewed as part of the drama of life rather than as merely the intermission. Many people, unfortunately, view it as the intermission. Consequently, apartments are decorated in a just-passing-through style instead of being designed to reflect the taste and personality of the occupant. As one woman said, "I've postponed buying furniture, putting up pictures, and even investing in good dishes. I chose to wait for Prince Charming to appear. Now five years have passed, and I realize my apartment is only a skeleton of who I am."

That was a turning point for this woman. She began to take an interest in making her apartment a home that reflected her likes and dislikes.

Being fully human has nothing to do with whether one is married or single. It has to do with how he lives his life. If he wants to be married but isn't, he must face the unfulfilled hopes so that he's able to live his todays more fully. If the person is choosing the single life-style, as more and more people are today, still he must deal with the dreams other people had for his life so that he can respond to his own goals.

How we cope with disappointment is related to how we deal with loss and expectations. Success and failure are often described in the eyes of others—mother, father, boss, peers, and so forth. Our fears of not living up to both spoken and unspoken expectations can make our lives a prison. We live on the knife-edge of apprehension until we choose to make singleness an opportunity for personal growth. Growth begins when we can honestly ask ourselves some searching questions:

1. What is your definition of success?
2. Who gives it to you?
3. What are your expectations of God in the painful valleys of your life?
4. Are you open to what God gives as appropriate, or must he follow your plan?
5. Do you try to block your growth by avoiding any precise picture of yourself? As long as your self-perception is vague, you can't realistically face your own expectations.
6. Look at the expectations you have for others. Do you

take responsibility for the part you play in things; or do you usually assume the role of poor, innocent victim?

   7. Evaluate your current perception of the following:
      a. Your career
      b. Personal habits
      c. Friendships
      d. Parents
      e. Yourself.

   8. As best you understand them, what are both the advantages and disadvantages of being a Christian single adult in today's world?

The first time one feels panic at the thought of being single is not the time to give up. Rather, it's the time for celebration. This may be his first real opportunity to grow and nurture his self-esteem. Panic may be the result the first time he asks himself searching questions.

The "How come you're not married?" question, when asked, seems to have a subtle, nonspoken "Is there something wrong with you?" attached to it. Charlotte, a woman of twenty-six, reacted strongly when people asked that question. She felt caught in a double bind with no way out. If she responded with explanations, the inquirer looked at her with pity. If she said she favored pursuing her career and education over marriage, it was assumed that she was selfish, unemotional, incomplete, and cold.

To show how much Charlotte had come to believe what others said, when she'd meet a single man for the first time, she would wonder, *What's wrong with you? Prove you're not some emotional freak.* Slowly she came to realize that she not only bought society's stereotypes; she secretly believed something must be wrong with her. Her self-contempt showed itself in ulcers.

This devaluation occurs at significant times in a single person's life, usually when it's least expected. The early twenties is the time of the first real gut-level panic, but some rationalize by saying, "There's still plenty of time left." As soon as a person rounds the corner of twenty-five, it again blazes through the heartstrings: "Better hurry and meet someone. Thirty isn't *that* far away." The thirtieth birthday can be a self-torturing experience if the person has postponed living while looking for a mate. Even if he's made peace with himself about not marrying, there's recognition that he's getting older and that the "right one" hasn't appeared yet. A low self-image may emerge, and the question of marriage is reevaluated. As one man pursuing forty said, "I honestly haven't wanted to marry, but now I secretly wonder if something is wrong with me."

Janice, a woman in her early thirties, said, "I feel like I've missed something. I'm not sure what; but the empty, half-a-person feeling is there."

Our Western culture has accented the "must be married" syndrome and, consequently, hasn't encouraged people to explore their identities. As one who is ministering to single adults, you will have to face your own myths about what it means to be single. Certainly, there are singles who are insecure, overly dependent, and aggressively searching for the "one and only." They fail to see themselves as whole, complete people; so they become self-effacing, depressed, and self-contemptuous. But there are others who are becoming more self-confident and self-reliant. They're looking at singlehood as a unique opportunity to pursue goals, careers, friendships, and interests. These single adults learn to take risks, greet change as an opportunity to learn, and get to know themselves as individuals, not stereotypes.

If you're willing to be involved in someone's struggle to become more of who he or she is, you will also be examining your own belief in stereotypes. Your response to the following questions shapes how you view the single experience.

1.   Do you believe that marriage will solve all problems? Whether married or single, you alone have responsibility for your life. Even if you're intimately related to a person, self-esteem is not something someone else can give you. In trying to find the "one and only," you sometimes not only degrade yourself; you overlook other people and experiences. Such a search requires enormous energy, and usually you generate so much tension and aggression within yourself that you drive people away.

2.   Is marriage a need or a want? If it's a want, you can deal with the disappointment. If it's a need, your desperation forces you to shortchange yourself and burden someone with shoulds, oughts, and demands impossible to fill. You give up seeing a person as real. Certainly, intellectually you may be able to recognize this. Integrating it emotionally is much more difficult and time-consuming. You begin with starting to cultivate your own interests and personality. When you learn to take care of yourself well, physically and emotionally, you can give up your fantasy of marriage as a cure-all.

"How come you're not married?" does not have to be a value judgment unless single adults make it one. Living single can be a time of potential or panic. How we live it is up to us!

3 Life is Problem-solving

I remember a client I'll call Sarah. At a crucial time in her midforties, she entered counseling depressed that her life was a constant series of mishaps. She'd experienced job losses, the death of relationships, and what she called "unbearable hardships." Now she was trying to fit the pieces of her life together, but she felt helpless and alone. Sarah was certain that if she just had faith enough and worked hard enough, conflicts and pressures would cease. "On good days," she said, "I feel tense and uptight. On my bad days, I'm terror-stricken, lonely, and depressed." Sarah spent much of her time punishing herself for what she didn't like about herself.

Finally realizing that her life was hers, warts and all, Sarah worked to a different point. "Perhaps," she said, "I can live with the problems and uncertainties of life if you can offer a 'reason' as to why it's this way." Like Job, who suffered unbearably, she hoped there would be some purpose for the calamities of life. Sarah wanted fairness, rightness, or, at a minimum, an explanation! No one promised that life would be problem free, even for the Christian. The promise was that God would be with us through all of life's experiences!

Sarah "kicked and screamed" the whole way as she worked

33

to face that she would not be perfect. She too would be on the inevitable journey of learning to accept herself, complete with feelings, thoughts, and actions. As Sarah came to assume responsibility for her life and to understand how she manipulated people to take care of her, she experienced a sense of freedom and security. Life would always be a process of problem-solving, but she wanted to learn to like and accept herself. Learning to live as an imperfect pedestrian is a never-ending journey.

Sarah's story is not unusual. Each of us must face the ambiguities of adulthood. To face them with another person, a client must perceive and receive a communication from you. That message will either convey that you understand and accept him where he is, *or* it will mean that you expect him to be where *you* are. Growth occurs if you're "with" a client; anger and resentment result if you want him to meet your agenda. There are several ways to communicate that you're able to accept someone at his point of pain or questioning.

Positive Responses

1. Ask appropriate questions—"What's happening?" or "What did you do (or say)?"

2. Show interest and express concern.

3. Educate the client to the fact that life is problem-solving.

Negative Responses

1. Don't say, "Why did you do that?" or "That was a silly response."

2. Don't tell the client to "shape up."

3. Don't imply that this situation will improve "if only . . ."

When you express a sense of humor, suggest new options, and slowly build a trusting relationship by respecting boundaries and limitations, then you've said in effect, "I'm with you. I hear you."

That's a beginning. But within the first few minutes together, you'll begin to get a glimpse of how a person sees himself. Looking for cues to self-hate and depression is a link in the chain to growing self-esteem. Self-hate might be expressed in statements such as:

"I don't deserve it."

"I feel good, but I know it won't last."

"Everyone I love leaves me."

"I'm afraid to trust."

"I've felt guilty all my life."

"I shouldn't feel this way."

The ultimate fear is expressed in silence. Silence makes many statements, but one of the most common is the fear of rejection. You hear it represented in statements such as:

"I don't know the right thing to say."

"I might be wrong if I say what I think."

"If I let people know me (including you), they might not like me."

"I'll sound stupid."

"It's silly for me to have these feelings."

"Christians shouldn't feel this way."

"I'm afraid—others have left when I told them about myself."

Rather than judging a person's silence, it's more useful to accept his fears and be curious enough to ask:

"What's scary about letting me know a little of you?"

"You're the expert on your life, not me. Is it tough to believe I'm interested in you?"

"Perfect people make me uncomfortable. I'm glad neither

of us is. What are you afraid might happen if you tell me what's happening?"

"Take your time. Talking to another person can be scary."

These statements are an assurance that you respect the person and his boundaries but are interested. Defenses are healthy; so it's important to affirm the person's decision to ascertain whether he can trust you.

Silence is not the only indicator to look for in the first few minutes. It's necessary to make some assessment about whether a person is depressed. A high degree of depression would indicate that a referral to a trained professional is appropriate. Mild depression might be indicated in a high frequency of such statements as:

"I'm low."

"I can't sleep."

"I'm crying more than usual."

"I have trouble getting up in the morning."

"I'm restless."

"I don't feel anything; I'm numb."

"I constantly feel irritable."

Everyone is haunted by a potential that is God-given. We generally are depressed over our failure to reach our (and others') expectations. Depression is a reaction to stress. Many people who are single are stepping back from the limits of day-to-day living in order to examine who and where they are. It can be a time of anxiety, but it can also be a time of exhilaration.

When people use energy for self-evaluation, they sometimes have little left for involvement with other people and activities. Energy is like currency—there's just so much. When it's gone, it must be replenished. During times of self-examination I've heard this criticism: "Singles are too selfish." The implication is that learning to become whole individuals is a waste of time. Yet only when we're emotionally healthy can we like ourselves. God didn't make perfect people; he made human beings and encouraged us to mature.

When we criticize others for being less than we think they can be, we must remember that the more righteous *we* become, the deeper we're in sin! Granted, there are those who are selfish; but that's not a synonym for single. And there are occasions of intense stress, such as after a divorce or the death of a spouse, when all energy must be devoted to surviving the loss. That's not selfish. That's a recognition that we have no choice but to learn to take care of ourselves.

Wholeness is a never-ending part of the developmental cycle. It occurs as a challenge during each of life's transition stages. We must remember that old struggles seldom get resolved forever. Old patterns surface during times of stress. In our journey toward wholeness, we'll have to begin again and again as we face hurdles along the way.

During one of the singles seminars at South Main Baptist Church, we talked about ground rules for learning to like yourself. The dialogue began with the wisdom of a bumper sticker: "The truth will set you free, but first it will make you miserable." Following are some of the rules that formed a "singles contract":

1. You have the privilege not to be involved with people or activities that compromise your feelings or values.

2. You have the privilege to make mistakes and to try to learn from them.

3. You have the privilege to renegotiate relationships as you discover the need for doing so.

4. You have the privilege not to have to be perfect. An occasional admitted mistake will signal your humanness.

5.   You have the privilege not to have to explain your decisions, thoughts, or feelings. It's appropriate to set boundaries.

6.   You have the privilege to grieve over losses in your own way.

7.   You have the privilege to say no, guilt-free.

8.   You have the privilege to look at the changes in your life and to claim what's replacing old patterns—the best antidote to avoid becoming cynical about change.

9.   You have the privilege to come to terms with your own limits and boundaries even if that means saying good-bye to certain people, jobs, or expectations.

10.   You have the privilege to fail. Failure is a disappointment, not a life issue.

11.   You have the privilege to listen to your feelings and learn from them.

12.   You have the privilege to be self-affirming. Give yourself credit for things you do to your satisfaction. Positive strokes to the psyche are as important as food to the body.

13.   You have the privilege to change the focus of your life from living in the past or future to living in the present.

14.   You have the privilege to accept forgiveness from God and from yourself.

15.   You don't have the privilege to
   a.   Be responsible for the disappointment of everyone you know
   b.   Postpone living for a magic happily-ever-after time
   c.   Abdicate responsibility for your decisions
   d.   Avoid getting to know yourself
   e.   Give up.

Along with the contract, a road map for focusing on strengths was offered. It was amazing how many people focused on weaknesses and were out of touch with their strengths. Consequently, the strengths checklist is provided here.

Focus on Strengths

1. List your positive strengths and accomplishments. Consider:

    a. Health
    b. Appearance
    c. Intelligence
    d. Sense of humor
    e. Family resources—parents, brothers, sisters, cousins, children, aunts, uncles, grandparents.
    f. Friends—who? How many?
    g. Education
    h. Positive life experiences
    i. Talents and gifts (music, writing, listening, athletic, art, and so forth)
    j. Common sense
    k. Interest in personal growth
    l. Awareness and use of cultural opportunities
    m. Awareness and use of social opportunities
    n. Awareness and use of educational opportunities
    o. Awareness and use of economic opportunities
    p. Awareness and use of leisuretime opportunities
    q. Capacity for introspection
    r. Capacity for self-control
    s. Capacity for self-discipline
    t. Ability to have fun
    u. Meaningfulness of faith.

2. List your goals for each area. Which area do you plan to actively concentrate on first?

    a. Renegotiate relationships

   b. Job
   c. Self
   d. Family
   e. Church-related
   f. Professional counseling.

   3.   Where would you like to be six months from now? What steps do you plan to take to get there?

   When the single finds the signature that is unique to his life, he can begin to keep company with the world within the context of wholeness. He doesn't have to run or live in a fantasy world. He can celebrate life as he finds it. Surely Christ taught us a message of wholeness and of his availability as we opcn ourselves to it.

4 Creative Loneliness

One group of singles lingered after a seminar to talk about the common thread between them—living alone and being lonely. After what seemed like a long, endless time, John broke the silence with, "Oh, God, how I've prayed for an end to loneliness." He slouched forward in his chair with his arms dangling at his sides, exhausted. John looked very tired after describing his world of lonely evenings. Memories of his wife haunted him—their twenty-year marriage, the fun years, the difficult times, and especially the car accident that took her life.

John described his typical day: "I go to work, busily filling every moment with activity. But by 3:30 I have a case of dreads. Five o'clock will come; I can't prevent it. Then I aimlessly wander to the house that contains so much of Anne's touch. I lie in bed fighting thoughts that it is over for me. My heart beats twice as fast as normal, and I wonder if I'll die from loneliness. I want to feel like I did before Anne died—complete, interested in people, active in the community, and looking forward to tomorrow. My life is bits and pieces of painful memories. I feel like life has stopped, and I don't have the energy or the desire to start again."

John, as a recent widower, confronted the loneliness that

is a result of losing someone we love. The period of new loss is an intense process of pain and reflection. Being alone is part of the healing process that comes when we sort out our lives, grieve over the loss of a love, and begin rebuilding.

But his story represented only one of the powerful forms of loneliness. June, a woman in her late thirties, shared her own struggle with loneliness: "I'm not grieving over anyone because there's not anyone in my life who's as significant as Anne was to you. I'm not married. I wanted to be, but I have started dealing with the reality that I may never be. The pangs of terror I feel in my lonely times come when I least expect them. Like the other day—I attended a symphony, but had no one to share the magic moments with. I start cringing when the holiday seasons approach. Everyone seems so happy and surrounded by family. I feel myself sinking into lonely isolation; but at the bottom of my emptiness, I wonder if their happiness is real. I question whether holidays are ever plastic and pretense for the many who applaud their approach. I still ache to have someone share my world and care about me. Just to have the realization that someone wants me home with him at night . . ."

Her voice trailed off into silent reflection. June was more than an acquaintance of what some call the disease of loneliness. As the group of five continued to share their battles and their battlescars, it became clear that loneliness is no respecter of persons.

Two people who made similar choices expressed their fears: Ted, a man in his late twenties, explained his dilemma. "I moved here from the East and have found the adjustment difficult. For one thing, there's a pressure here to marry, or people begin to look for reasons why you're not. People raise their eyebrows and wonder whether I dislike girls, am impotent, am a homosexual, or have zero personality. Actually, in my family, no one married until their early thirties. We grew up thinking that after college, a person explores career opportunities, meets a variety of people, and learns to stand on his own two feet. Sure, I'm lonely; but it comes from feeling misunderstood. I'd like to marry someday, but I'm not living my life to meet others' expectations. But when I have bad days at work or feel low, that nauseating loneliness of feeling like no one understands and accepts me is unbearable."

Joy had a similar experience. She wasn't certain that she even wanted to be married. She'd experienced the problems and frustrations of her parents' marriage and wasn't sure she wanted to commit her time and energy to someone in marriage. Joy wasn't certain marriage was intended for everyone. So, as she sorted out her life direction, she put energy into education and her career.

"I'm a social worker with an agency in town," she explained. "I thoroughly enjoy my job, but I feel isolated and lonely. People become case numbers; staff meetings are gripe sessions; there's little time to get to know anyone. Some days I feel lonely for someone to care about *my* needs. I give and give, yet have no time to form relationships. I'm surrounded with people, but acutely lonely. The most difficult times are when I make decisions concerning placement of children in foster homes. The parents are hostile; the children are upset; lawyers apply pressure—the loneliness of making those kinds of decisions and standing alone with them—I shudder to recall those moments."

Although they had different experiences, Joy could understand how the pain and fear of loneliness motivated Eva to run into relationships with any man available.

Eva knew the pangs of loneliness in her marriage; but, as with most people, she was not prepared for their sharpness

in divorce. The emotional whirlwind after the death of a
marriage was not something Eva was prepared to enter.
Acute loneliness and her fear of memories drove her to
search for anyone who could ease her pain. Premature relationships became her way to run from herself and the unbearable grief she encountered on the other side of marriage.
After a series of affairs, Eva described her feelings: "I was
so frightened, so lonely, that after the divorce I couldn't
tolerate being alone. I frantically filled my calendar with
people and activities, hoping to outrun myself. I ached for
someone to touch me, whether he truly cared for me or
not—anything to prove to myself that I wasn't alone.

"Eventually, I discovered that those relationships didn't
cure my nagging loneliness. In fact, they began to accentuate
my emptiness. I couldn't stand myself; I hated my inability
to stand on my own two feet and deal with my life. I entered
a counseling process and began to learn to take care of myself. I grieved over the death of my marriage. I allowed
my anger to surface, then learned from its lessons within
the counseling experience. One-night stands were not an
answer, but I'm trying to learn from those past experiences.
I've had all-consuming guilt trips to deal with, but I'm trying
to move through them. There are things I regret, but I can't
build a life on past regrets."

Loneliness is a companion to singles but to others as well.
Christian and non-Christian, male and female, parent and
child, husband and wife—whatever the role, each of us journeys through life with varying degrees of loneliness. For
many it's a destructive experience. We've learned to fear
loneliness; and we feel a sense of rejection, frustration, and
anger if we struggle with lonely moments. One woman
wrote, "During the loneliest time of my life, I walked to
the edge of the sea and stopped. I wished I could have kept

on walking and withdrawn from myself and the world. I was tempted by the seductive, flirting waves. It seemed a way out. But I turned my back to the expanse of water and moonlight. I walked back over my newly made footprints in the sand."

This woman faced the moment when she made her choice—retreat or turn around and face life as it is. Each of us has such choices; and we make them time and again, in both covert and overt ways.

As you talk with people about loneliness, they may tend to downplay its significance in their lives. After all, a common response to the lonely is "Get busy. What's wrong with you?" That type of comment triggers instant distress!

It would be helpful for you to determine what "I'm lonely" means to each individual. Some say lonely when they mean isolated. There's a distinct difference between being lonely and alone. Frequently, people are lonely in a crowd, while others who live alone aren't crippled by loneliness. On other occasions a person may equate loneliness and depression as synonymous. However, depression is immobilizing. Depressed persons feel sapped of energy; and if they're really down, they just don't feel like doing anything.

Loneliness, however, can motivate. One may feel a sharp, aching sensation such as in occasions of severe grief, separation, or divorce. It can be a dull, stressful feeling that seems to tug at the emotions and physical well-being. But it does have a driving power. People try to run away, surround themselves with people, write, talk on the phone, enter countless new relationships, get married, join committees, and so forth—all motivated by the power in loneliness.

There is generally a message in loneliness—a painful awareness, perhaps, but a signal to ourselves. Most of us run from our fear of what that signal is and how it will affect us. Yet the experience itself will not be as problematic as what occurs when we run from it.

It's important to discover what patterns encompass our lonely times. Perhaps constant blues on holidays or at the end of the day is a hint to do things differently. Perhaps the lonely feelings most frequently occur when our expectations are frustrated. Our society emphasizes success; and that means making it in careers, in relationships, in sports, and in entertaining. It symbolizes fitting in, being popular, having people like and want to be with us. Our disappointment in not reaching expectations, whether our own or other people's, leaves us frightened, confused, angry, and unprepared to deal with painful reality.

As William Sadler has suggested, we can experience loneliness from many sources. It may be that we're cut off in relationship to God, another person, a tradition, a family or other group, a meaning for life, or a need for a type of activity. If all of these types are involved, the stress may motivate an eventual breakdown.

The pervasiveness and intensity of loneliness in our society demands that we learn its source and take steps to deal with it. But, equally importantly, we must learn to develop inner resources that are necessary for us to deal with the lonely times that catch us off guard.

The source of loneliness has much to do with how the person chooses to respond to it. One person may move from loneliness to depression and become immobile; another may react to lonely times with anger and become destructive. During times of separation from ourselves and from God, we're aware of the cosmic loneliness of being human. That realization prompts us to become overly dependent on others, seek conformity, and strive for overachievement. But being lonely is not always a separateness from persons, groups, or heritage. Often our personal shyness, a desire for love but a fear of it, motivates our lonely moments. Do not fault someone for being lonely—it is a natural condition of being human and experiencing loss.

Instead, learn how to be responsive. You don't preach an impromptu sermon on God when the loneliness stems from missing someone who has died. You don't greet an international student with the pluses of American life if he is grieving over the loss of his homeland. You don't encourage someone to make friends when he fears that he's drifted away from God.

By having a person tell his story, try to discover the implications of his loneliness. In addition, help him discover his fears about being lonely so that he won't sabotage moments that can be used for self-discovery. When people are ready, I offer a series of questions that can make lonely spaces a self-directed pilgrimage.

1. What's scary about being lonely?

2. What messages (verbal and nonverbal) did you receive in the family you grew up in? Did you feel lonely in your family? How did you deal with loneliness?

3. Describe your significant relationships. Who is important in your life?

4. Who or what do you feel separated from?

5. What emotions do you feel when you say "I'm lonely"?

6. Who are your closest friends? What qualities does each have that you admire?

7. What are your relationships with business associates like?

8. What triggers your loneliness (time of day, certain events, and so forth)?

9. When did you last feel lonely? What triggered the

feeling? How did you deal with it?

   10.   How do you set yourself up to feel lonely?

   11.   How could you deal with or improve the situation?

   12.   What are your expectations for yourself during lonely times? for friends? for God?

   13.   What positive use can you create for lonely times?

After learning the type of loneliness and how a person handles it, you can help a person update his image of himself.

   1.   List fifteen words that characterize you.

   2.   What are your current priorities?

   3.   What are your values as you presently understand them?

   4.   What do you like about yourself?

   5.   What would you like to change? How will you go about it?

   6.   List three things you've done to your satisfaction in your life.

   7.   List one goal for yourself over the next six months.

   8. How will you take responsibility for dealing with your lonely moments?

   9.   What risks can you take to claim your own personhood without giving singlehood a rank of second-class citizen? (Learn to eat out alone, go to a movie alone, invite people to your place for dinner, and so forth.)

These are merely sample questions, but they give you an idea of the complexity of loneliness. Being available as a person who tries to understand is the first step toward helping. Then you can work with the options available to deal with the particular cause. Lonely spaces can become times to reevaluate relationships, develop inner resources, and respond in faith in God.

A word of caution. This is not a cure-all, but a beginning. Often the struggle to deal with the underlying issues—di-

vorce, widowhood, learning to live creatively as a single—
is itself a journey that involves a process of counseling. Loneliness is not comfortable. In fact, it can become a disease
that affects physical and emotional health. Even creative
loneliness has a price tag of painful self-awareness!

5 Mirror to Your World: Time, Money, Health

We have inner and outer time clocks that record the story of our lives. Although the heart and mind are not divided into minutes, days, and weeks, they record events according to intensity rather than duration. Emotional experiences, whether loving or painful, may be accorded a very prominent position in memory.

Our outer time clock is punctuated by guideposts from one stage of life to the next. How the hours of our days are structured helps determine how we work with turbulent transitions. Each person responds to crisis in part according to how society defines and values it. In our society, rites of passage are often blurred and mechanical. Consequently, marriages, credit cards, mortgages, driver's licenses, and so forth are signs of full responsibility. Adulthood is often measured in success, which is defined as having money, health, and no identity crisis. The problem with this definition is that trauma is translated as shame and despair—when, in fact, transitions signal growth and potential creativity. So our "maturity cards" and how we use them can be a nonverbal announcement of what's going on inside.

Claire, a woman in her midthirties, unmarried and childless, came into my office. She arrived at the first session with her wheat-colored hair windblown and her clothes disheveled. Her body posture announced her depression. About twenty-five pounds overweight, Claire was absorbed in her low self-esteem and disappointment. If she could have jumped out of her body and watched herself, she would have immediately noticed how her appearance proclaimed her unhappiness.

Her private self imprisoned her spontaneity and guarded her self-hatred from others. Claire was afraid to let anyone see her own degrading self-image, so she blocked from relationships her tenderness, dreams, goals, and even her sense of being human. She'd gone from relationship to relationship, each one ending with tears, recrimination, and the feeling that permanence in love was unrealistic. As she walked into my office that first time, Claire was confused, inaccessible, and afraid, yet pleased that no one really knew her. Her behavior and the things she disliked about herself had been ganging up on her for months, but when she spent an entire night sobbing alone she decided to take a positive step. She wasn't certain she knew herself anymore; or perhaps she knew more than she could assimilate.

Claire's story is not unusual from the standpoint that how we relate to time, health, and money reflects our image of ourselves. She spent little time alone unless she had something to do—reading, talking on the phone, or drinking. Claire didn't like herself, so why would she want to spend time with her own ideas, thoughts, and feelings? There was no structure to her life in the way that commas, periods, and exclamation and question marks provide boundaries for language.

A typical morning would begin with her waking up late and rushing to work without breakfast. Claire would grab coffee breaks if and when she could, often eat lunch late, and leave the office dreading the evening. She'd enter an apartment full of unopened boxes and sparsely decorated rooms. Clothes draped on chairs, an untidy kitchen, and pictureless walls characterized her "home." Its condition was a reflection of how she felt about herself—unsettled, confused, unsure of what she wanted or how to get there. The lack of structure suggested her susceptibility to sudden mood shifts and lack of boundaries.

Her use of physical space was one indication of how she both postponed living and detested her present circumstances. But Claire's emotional space was a void as well. There were no people she could call friends. She had acquaintances in abundance, but by choice she lived in a web of isolation. She feared intimacy more than she did the pain of loneliness. There was no warmth or support system; and her management of her appearance, house, and time reflected that emotional mood.

How Claire used her financial assets was another clue to her self-image. People can "act out" with money just as they do with other things. For instance, it's not uncommon for someone living with divorce to deal with his anxiety by going on spending sprees. The purchase of clothes is a quick attempt to try to feel better on the outside, even if grieving inside.

At any rate, how money is used indicates current values, priorities, and needs. The less confident and more threatened we feel, the less we tend to logically weigh alternatives and make choices. Instead, we opt for a reduction in anxiety and pseudosafety. Singles must learn not only to provide for themselves, but also to protect themselves.

Claire had not reconciled with herself that she would assume responsibility for herself and her choices. Initially, she was intent on blaming others while she acted out her distance in her appearance and in wild spending patterns. Often she'd be overdrawn at the bank and feel the ambivalence of shame and self-affirmation that she was "good for nothing," after all. Claire set herself up to feel worthless by overspending.

As you work with singles, you will find the outward signs of esteem related to self-management. As Claire worked through her personal problems, she began to lose weight and to take an interest in the appearance of her apartment, as well as herself. She learned to take seriously the merits of a good diet, eating habits on a specific time structure, sleep, and exercise. No longer did she fall into bed at 2:30 A.M. and struggle to get up at 6:30. She set bedtimes and stuck with them. When insomnia made sleep impossible, rather than brood about it, she used the time. During those nights Claire would sew, clean house, read, or even try her new hobby of painting. The important thing was that she took more responsibility for herself, and that was reflected in these other areas.

How you relate to singles depends on how you understand the messages hidden in the use of time, money, and health. In some cases, irresponsible choices may be symptomatic of what's occurring in the private, inner life of the person. In other cases, it may represent the need for an educational process.

Someone who has lost a mate may need to learn new skills when it comes to budgeting, time, and health management. Your church can draw from its membership people who can conduct seminars on budgets, taxes, provision for emergencies, how to achieve credit, tithing, and so forth. This would be a useful contribution to the lives of all the people in your church.

6 How Do You Make Decisions?

Somewhere along the way, many of us learned to devalue ourselves. It was a very subtle learning experience, but a powerful one. We learned that to listen to our feelings, trust our thoughts, and take care of ourselves was self-indulgent. So instead of getting to know ourselves, we felt guilty. Certainly, there are those who give the impression of conceit and self-centeredness. But often these are the ones who are the most insecure of all. Then there are those who caution that time spent on self is sinful. Yet Jesus openly met his own needs in order to have the strength to respond to others.

How you feel about yourself determines the quality of your relationships with other people. If you're not in touch with your own needs, interests, and boundaries, you may be threatened by the pendulum of emotions that single adults work through. So before you read any further, ask yourself the following questions about your own life:

1.   In what ways are you unique?

2.   Who knows you the best?

3.   How much of the public mask you wear is really what you're like on the inside?

4.   For what audience do you perform?

5.   What people control your life? Is there someone whose affirmation you seek?

6.   When are you most self-critical?

7.   What ideal are you chasing?

8.   What is the meaning of time for you? Where have you come from? Where are you going? How will you decide?

9.   What patterns do you repeat even though they are frustrating to you?

10.   How do you get your way with other people (become a salesman, victim, martyr; become self-righteous, guilt-ridden, and so forth)?

11.   How often do you say "I can't" when you mean "I won't"?

12.   Recall the times when you've felt the lowest. How did you make the situation worse? better?

13.   How do you like to spend your time?

14.   When was the last time you took an inventory of your strengths and lesser strengths?

15.   How do you make decisions? Do you expect others to use the same process in making them?

16.   Have you ever learned from mistakes and failures, or do you block growth areas and subtly encourage others to "be perfect"?

Helping someone learn how to make decisions and think for himself is an investment in his future.

Carol was so accustomed to having other people make decisions for her that she hadn't learned how to make them for herself. Characteristically, when faced with a difficult decision, Carol took an opinion poll from family and friends. Laughingly, she later recalled that she made her choices based on which side had the highest vote. Whenever she was involved in a meaningful dating relationship, Carol opted to meet real or imagined expectations of her boyfriend. She agreed with anything to "make him happy," including decisions made from his perspective and not always in her best interest. Often decisions were made by default.

She recounted one situation: "I couldn't decide whether to spend the Labor Day weekend at Glorieta or go to Galveston and get some sun. Actually, I didn't do either one—I dreamed about both all weekend while I stayed home." The decision was made, for making no decision is in actuality making a decision! Before Carol learned how to take responsibility for herself, she'd lived the cycles of roles. In some instances, she was the victim of all that happened in her life. At other times she vacillated between manipulating and being manipulated, as she sought to give someone else the responsibility for her life.

When she sought counseling, she hoped I would tell her whether or not to change careers. Since I was not inclined to encourage an unhealthy dependency relationship with her, I explained that I wouldn't accept responsibility for her life decisions. After we established a contract in which she'd learn *how* to make her own decisions, she explored and worked with her anger, disappointment, and need to hook people to take care of her.

It costs to be fully human. Old forms of behavior must be shed for new ones; the search for security becomes less the goal; courting questions and doubts becomes the price for awareness.

Unfortunately, how we make the little decisions we face is translated into how we make life decisions. People marry, create friendships, select careers, and join a church using the same method—even the "default decision."

Generally, the more we hear a concept or idea, the less we deal with it. The art of decision making has been preached, taught, lectured, sold, and bumper-stickered to death! So we work to avoid confrontation with ourselves and a powerful fact: We may have to learn to examine our viewpoint, learn new skills, even enter a counseling process in order to discover new ways of relating.

There is a process of decision making that a person can learn to follow if he's willing to give up old patterns. Although it appears simplistic in written form, it's quite difficult to adapt. It requires practice and commitment to facing inner fears. This checklist may be helpful for your client:

1. Be aware of the problem. Often we give up our power of options by mentally blocking the existence of a problem. One woman, now divorced, recalled that she had a clue of potential marriage problems even before the wedding. After she and Todd, her fiancé, left the courthouse with their newly purchased marriage license, he fainted! Another woman twenty years later recalled the anxiety she felt about her impending marriage. She spent most of her wedding day in the bathroom vomiting. She weakly made it through the ceremony that night, but wondered what message her body was trying to give her! Another response to the same problem is evident with the person who waves the banner of "There's nothing I can do about it." Those famous last words have closed the door on many a potential option for resolving a problem before it grew into a crisis.

2. A person must recognize his values, priorities, and time frame at the time of a potential problem. If you're moving through a grief process, have left your job, or are emotionally at low ebb, it isn't wise to make crucial life decisions. In fact, it's important not to pressure yourself into decisions to please other people or your own time schedule. One man, after the recent death of his mate, made a decision that he wouldn't hurt after two months! Grief saps energy and is uncomfortable, but it's necessary in order to say good-bye and reconstruct life.

Decisions are not made in a vacuum. Our values and priorities influence even our small decisions. List ten priorities you have and determine how they correspond to your physical, mental, spiritual, and material values. But don't stop there. Now discover how much time is given to each priority. Sometimes we only give them lip service! Time allotment is a key to which priorities are really being lived out.

3.   Look at your goals; discover the resources available to meet those goals; and set a time limit for the decision. Often we relax in knowing that we're *going* to make a decision—sometime between now and death. Certainly all decisions are made with less than total information. Sometimes we can only brainstorm about options, wonder through "what if" questions, and then *decide*.

4.   After you've examined your options and selected your choice, let your physical and emotional warning system send you messages. Listen to your feelings and to your nagging back or stomachaches! Your mind may logically lead you through a decision-making process, but your stomach will tell you how the choice feels! Gut feelings can be friends if you learn to listen and trust. Frequently, they prod you into taking risks that your head has rationalized away. We think about what others will say or what failure would mean and often don't grow into risk taking. Listen, and evaluate with the total picture.

5.   Have an alternative option to pursue if you discover that your first choice is not possible or appropriate, or if additional information is gathered which makes a second choice more feasible. Feedback with another person is often useful not only to widen your perspective but also to clarify your position. When you put into words what has until now been mental activity, you are called on to clarify your direction.

6. If you've moved this far, then make a commitment to follow through. A decision to be implemented sometime between now and death isn't definitive enough! Explore ways you can make things happen rather than majoring exclusively on the negative. Make the commitment and write down your goal, the problem, your choice to deal with it, how that will happen, and your time limit. Then date the card and save it. You will be able to look back over past decisions and compare how you relate to making changes now! You'll also discover that people generally do the best they can given the circumstances, available information, and personal emotional climate at the time. That realization is an encouragement to let go of the twenty-twenty hindsight that is used to berate yourself.

7. Make only decisions that are yours to make. Hopefully, you won't get so carried away that you attempt to run other people's lives! A fine line, but a powerful one, exists between advice and concern for other people.

Lastly, if your decision isn't working for you, reevaluate and chunk it. I'm reminded of a school counselor who heard a colleague say, "No one should change his mind once he's made it up. We should be committed to our decisions." This particular school counselor spoke up and with one comment ended the discussion. He said, "Interesting. A year ago I was dealing with the upheaval of my divorce. I decided to end the tormenting pain by attempting suicide. But I never carried it out. Sure would hate to have been obligated to make good on that decision." The meeting ended; the perspective was clearer then. This counselor did what is so difficult for many of us: He stood up for himself and didn't become paralyzed by others' opinions.

If you're dealing with someone who has never made decisions for himself, encourage him by focusing on his past successes. Hear the fears, but affirm those strengths the person sees in himself. If he isn't in touch with his gifts and talents, begin there. Help him discover his strengths.

On the other hand, if the person is contemplating several major decisions at once, your task may be to help him focus on one at a time. Too many changes within a short time period are highly stress producing. Physical and emotional well-being are jeopardized with frequent major changes!

We put equal energy into thinking positive or negative thoughts and making good or bad decisions. As we must learn to value ourselves, we need also to learn how to make decisions which reflect that growth.

Considerations for Times with Friends

7 Building Intimate Relationships

Intimacy begins within each of us. We tend to define it as something that occurs with another person, but it begins with love and acceptance of ourselves. It's our thoughts, hopes, dreams, and fantasies. Intimacy is emotional, spiritual, mental, and physical. It may, but does not have to, include sex.

Many times, people fight to loosen the rope of self-contempt they hold on themselves by seeking recognition from other people. Yet doing that doesn't alter their inner attitudes or toxic patterns of behavior. Regardless of age, each of us can learn to achieve greater self-intimacy. Look at the following comparisons with your client and help him discover his degree of intimacy with himself.

1. Do you assume responsibility for yourself, your needs, and your goals? Or do you use energy looking for someone to take care of you emotionally?

2. Do you share the thoughts and feelings you choose to share with whoever is important in your life? And do you say no to requests to share subjects that are private to you? Or do you feel guilty when you're unwilling to share certain aspects of your life?

3. Do you assume responsibility for your own growth and awareness? Or are you looking for someone to approve

of you, with the hope that their doing so will lead to greater self-acceptance?

4.   Do you live your todays and plan for tomorrow? Or do you live for tomorrow and postpone living today?

5.   Do you seek new experiences and initiate activities? Or do you wait for others to initiate activities while you passively wait, bored?

6.   Are you in touch with your strengths and talents? Or do you disclaim your gifts and accent what you don't like about yourself?

7.   Do you use anxiety and loneliness to motivate you into problem-solving? Or do you withdraw from yourself and other people?

8.   Do you view singlehood as an opportunity for growth? Or do you view yourself as a second-class citizen living between the times?

9.   Do you feel like an integrated, whole person? Or do you feel that your identity is fragmented into compart- ments of "acceptable" and "unacceptable"?

10.   Do you have the security and stability with yourself that comes with being nice to yourself? Or do you feel des- perate and directly or indirectly send the message "I want you to take care of me"?

Many people are paralyzed with fear at the thought of getting to know themselves. They silently question, *What if I discover something I don't want to know?* Yet the process of intimacy involves the road to self-discovery. Those without it try to fill their lives with quantity experiences and relation- ships, and they sacrifice the depth and quality available to them. However, none of us can indefinitely escape the pain of our anxieties. If we retreat into ourselves or into work, alcohol, drugs, or shallow relationships, our "solutions" give only temporary relief, if that.

Each of us has the choice—we can enter or retreat from

ourselves; we can grow or not grow. Intimacy within involves the self-discovery of what attitudes, behavior patterns, and meaning fit our uniqueness. Discovery comes as we move through life experiences as participants. By learning the consequences of our behavior, we learn what we do want and also what we don't want. Then we must develop our effectiveness in saying yes or no, depending on what's in the best interest of a healthy identity.

The ability to say no is essential in providing self and relationship well-being. The capacity to develop boundaries prevents fragmentation as well as overinvolvement. However, the other side is being able to say yes to people, experiences, and ourselves when doing so provides a richness in growth. The key is that each of us must learn to avoid intrusions that will negate inner intimacy. Anytime a person lives a life-style that violates his personal integrity, he victimizes himself. In so doing, he also remains vulnerable to manipulation and the demands of other people.

Staying in touch with our intimate selves is necessary in order to relate intimately with others. Only when we discover and act on our own likes, dislikes, boundaries, strengths, and limitations can we relate intimately to ourselves. And intimacy with another person begins with intimacy within ourselves!

Each person has a set of myths about what intimacy means. John, a man in his late twenties, listed the intimacy rules that govern his life.

1. An intimate is someone to take care of me.

2. Intimacy means thinking and feeling the same way about things. There's no difference between us.

3. Intimacy means giving up total freedom of thought.

4. If you love me, you're obligated to do whatever will make me happy.

5. You will take care of my insecurity needs.

6.   Intimacy is living happily.

7.   My intimate will deal with the anxieties that I can't cope with alone.

8.   Intimacy and sexuality are the same thing.

It's no wonder that John's relationships would deteriorate after a certain point. His eight rules were an excessive load for someone to carry.

Healthy intimacy is a way of relating in which two people are able to have closeness within the relationship while at the same time to have enough distance for unique identities. As such, each person has the support of being in the relationship, which also contributes to fulfilling potential.

Intimacy is a process that requires years. To develop acceptance and trust on a continuing basis requires time to integrate and assimilate the experiences between the two persons. Those relationships that are quickly and intensely intimate may have the feeling element, but time is necessary for the relationship to grow into a stable, enduring one.

Once again, how one relates to himself correlates with how one relates to an intimate. If Mary has patterns that prohibit reevaluation, risk taking, and emotionally taking care of herself, that will show up in the relationship. She'll become overly possessive and afraid to be spontaneous. She'll look to the relationship as the cure-all for frustration, insecurity, loneliness, and self-alienation. And her intimate will feel responsible for meeting her needs and for giving her an identity.

It won't work for long. The relationship will either blow up or begin slowly deteriorating. Those who learn to be self-reliant are more able to live with the ingredients necessary for intimacy. Those ingredients include:

1.   Ability to be flexible. The relationship sheds old, worn-out ways of relating for new ones. It's comparable to

our shedding of clothes when we outgrow them and replacing them with more mature, better-fitting ones.

2. Ability to make requests. You have the ability to ask what you want. No one has to second-guess you. Even when angry, you can request that your need be dealt with instead of making subtle, stinging stabs in the back.

3. Ability to see yourself as a whole person whom the relationship enhances instead of half a person looking for completeness.

4. Ability to understand that you and your intimate at times need emotional space, and that's natural. There's no value judgment on the relationship just because you want times alone.

5. Ability to allow a person his disappointments, fears, and insecurities without having to protect or change him.

6. Ability to appreciate the differences between you as well as the similarities.

7. The knowledge that intimacy means working on the relationship rather than taking it for granted.

8. Ability to assume responsibility for your personal growth and to accept your intimate's need to do the same.

9. Ability to use anger as the survival kit for crisis rather than pretending it isn't there. Healthy anger can mean improved communication and better relating.

10. Ability to negotiate, compromise, claim your feelings, and allow your intimate to do the same. You can accept that a person may feel differently than you do without that fact's meaning rejection.

11. Ability to relate to your intimate as he is rather than as you would like him to be.

12. Ability to accept that in order for relationships to grow, individuals must grow. Change can be a time of celebration and deeper commitment if you have an interdepen-

dent relationship rather than one that fosters clinging dependency.

It takes both people to be committed to the growth of a relationship. If one person is committed to multiple relationships, then the degree of intimacy is diminished. You don't have the time, energy, or emotional ingredients necessary to be intimately involved with the multitudes. Sometimes people will say that jumping from relationship to relationship is an attempt to gain intimacy. On the contrary, that's the best way to avoid it. Commitment, exclusiveness, conflict, and compromise are experienced in a low degree, if at all. When problems occur, relationships are ended. One-to-one intimacy means that a choice has been made to restrict some elements of individual freedom. (*Not* identity, however.) The price paid for relating to as many people as possible is *lack* of intimacy.

As someone involved with singles, you may have the privilege of being a part of a person's struggle to understand and achieve intimacy. That will also include a person's wanting to share sexual needs with that intimate person. Your involvement may take the form of helping the person decide *how* to deal with these needs. Telling a person *what* to do generally generates the kinds of feelings you would have if your father or mother came to your office and told you how to do your job, what to think, and what to feel for disobeying their rules. Helping a person respond to *how* he plans to deal with his sexual needs is a step in his accepting responsibility for his choices and their consequences. And that is the beginning of adulthood!

The beginning of intimacy occurs when one can look at the behavior patterns that put walls between himself and others. It begins when he tries out new patterns that help him to be self-reliant and to live his todays. It continues as he learns how to nurture a relationship without burdening it with needs. Intimacy is a process that is continual, for it takes years for each of us to learn to love ourselves, love our intimate, and integrate the experiences between the two of us.

8 The Art of Friendship

We live in a technical, urbanized world. Strangers meet without talking; people live with the grief of past hopes; one alone can quickly become saturated with boredom. Even in the church, people can look without seeing and hear without understanding. Some singles feel that their message is launched into a world that doesn't quite understand.

If you had a resumé of each single adult in your church, you would have sketches of events, honors, education, careers, children, and a reference to marital status. Even those who may be on their way to Nobel prizes don't list one of the most important sections—friendships.

The support system. An extended family. *The* family for single adults. I believe that to know someone, you must learn how he relates to his job, his past, and his present, but also how he relates to people. Who are his friends? How many? What kinds of relationships? Men and women, or friends only of one sex?

People are part of a network of relationships. And the interfacing of one with his friends, job, church, children, and anything else important in his life must be taken seriously.

None of us exists in a vacuum, even if we choose loneliness over the risk of intimacy. So when you're counseling with a person, be curious about who his friends are and how he relates to them. If there is no network of friends, the isolation can be deafening. If there are significant relationships, there may be an occasion when you want to observe how your client interacts with these people.

You will see people who either don't know the value of friendships or who have felt so burned in an intimate relationship that trust sounds like refuse of the past. You may see those in their early twenties still living for the promises they learned in childhood. They may be innocent of the knowledge of what life can offer. You will see people who were a product of the sixties. They may have learned first-hand about cynicism, war, and disillusionment. Such a person may have carried cynicism into believing the older generation made promises but delivered lies. Who does this person trust, if anyone? Other people may have matured to the philosophy of "OK, life is no bed of roses. It's tough. But let's quit blaming others and get to work." Whatever background these in their twenties have and whether they are unmarried, widowed, or divorced, who do they trust?

Move into the thirties. Some people may have been the protesters of a decade ago who became establishment and who now are divorced or widowed. Or they may have ridden out the sixties, touched only by the violence of the television screen. Perhaps they chose not to marry, regardless of whether the reason was career, identity, or opportunity. They may have been like many who believed in God and government—until Watergate. During the thirties people typically question values, priorities, and direction. Often the answer is disillusionment, unless the problems have been worked through. Who surrounds each of these individuals? What kinds of people make up their support system?

Some singles are in potentially the most creative age of

their lives—the forties. Identity questions, the meaning of life, death, success, failure—all are crucial issues. Many divorces occur during this time span. These individuals have lived through the tranquillity of the fifties, until the hard-rock boom exploded the status quo. They may have been mortified over events in the sixties. But now we're in the seventies and, according to some theologians, a rejuvenation of religion. But what if these persons are going through a divorce, facing life as a widow, or feeling that it's too late for marriage? Who are the friends that make up the extended family?

Of course, during the fifties and sixties everyone anticipates retirement, but hardly anyone is prepared for it. Mythology, the Social Security system, and the media have said that these persons are retired. But they may discover potential energy, vitality, interest in another career, sexual needs, and a resentment of people who imply that they're useless. If they're single, they may see some of their "family" die sooner than expected. They're aware of those who are depressed because of major illness or forced retirement. They may have been devotees of the Puritan work ethic. If so, meaningful work was their ticket to personal worthiness. They're too young to give up, but they must restructure their lives. Who are their friends?

As someone who has a caring interest in single adults, you need to know where each person is in more ways than just marital status. The simplistic generalizations I've made are not binding, but are given only to encourage curiosity about a person's significant relationships. Each of us has his own meanings for the road he travels. Healthy, creative friendships reinforce our self-image and teach us much about ourselves.

Your role as a minister or counselor may be to aid in self-discovery. Each of us has patterns of relating that can be healthy or destructive. Learning from those patterns gives a person the freedom to explore changes and to make decisions about his way of relating.

To begin with, a person can list his major life decisions and transitions. These could include decisions about which university to attend or whether to attend college at all; which career interest to pursue; which jobs to interview for, and the one he accepted; moving; marriage; divorce; and so forth. He may remember the times that were particularly growth inducing, but how did his friends play a part? Who were they? How did they respond? Was support, indifference, rejection offered? How did he relate to them during these periods?

Then have the person think of the traits, history, or experiences that someone would need to know in order to understand him. Friends can fill the need to be understood. Granted, if one's self-image is poor, he will guard his inner self by feeling that "if he knew me, he wouldn't like me." Even if his self-image is good, not everyone will like him. Hopefully, also, he doesn't feel as though he must have a relationship with everyone he meets! No one can have close friends unless he tells something about who he is and learns to give and receive feedback. When other people respond to what they hear him saying and how he communicates his message, he has a picture of himself that someone else has taken. Comparing how he sees himself with how a friend sees him gives him vital information that helps him grow and develop his potential for relating.

Friendship is important with people of the same sex, but is also vital with the opposite sex. Friends don't always have to be lovers! Pressure from the peer group often transforms what was a meaningful friendship into a less valuable relationship. Singles are aware of the pressure. A man and woman can't be seen together too many times before questions such as "How is it going?" and "Are you two serious?" start cropping up. I remember one incident in which a man and woman attended church together. The relationship between the two of them had been defined as a mutual friendship. One Sunday they stood in line to greet the pastor at the close of the service. As they shook hands with him, he quipped, "Have you two set the date?" The couple looked at him, stunned, speechless, and embarrassed!

When singles look at the opposite sex only as potential lovers, the friendship aspects diminish. This is especially true if one partner is not interested in becoming involved in a love relationship at the present time. If the message transmitted is "I'm looking for a husband/wife," then some people will automatically distance themselves. What's lost is a potential friendship that may provide nourishment, personal awareness, and fun. Everyone should give himself permission to have opposite-sex friendships that don't have to be "going somewhere permanent."

If your client is relating to someone in a significant love relationship, the temptation may be to withdraw from his circle of friends. Yet there may be times when he wants a good friend to share his laughter, tears, or conversation. And if his love relationship ends, he experiences both the grief of the loss and the isolation of having no support system.

We trap ourselves and we burden our intimate by placing all of our friendship needs on him. It's far healthier to have a pattern of relating that includes close friends, acquaintances, potential friends, and even people we may choose not to have as friends.

In all relationships, there is the dichotomy of trying to live with autonomy while having dependency needs.

Whether the question concerns same- or opposite-sex friendships, there are guidelines that may be helpful in cultivating healthy relationships. You may want to discuss them with your client.

1. Talk with your friend about expectations for the relationship. Is one of you set up always to be the listener, or is the relationship a mutual give-and-take? Especially in men-women friendships, clarify what the relationship is and what it is not.

2. Talk about boundaries. There may be some areas of your life you wish not to discuss. Talking about your preference helps your friend not to interpret your boundary as rejection.

3. Let your friend know that you will make requests when you have them, rather than playing a mind-reading game with each other.

4. Talk about your freedom to feel, think, and react differently to situations. Doing so doesn't have to be a reflection on the relationship.

5. Set aside time periodically to update your image of each other.

6. Learn to listen, communicate your feelings, and dialogue with your friend.

7. Give your friend room to grow, and allow him privacy when he wants it.

8. Don't make promises you can't keep, especially ones that focus on future times that you can't predict. You can't always promise feelings.

Singles already know the obvious: Some relationships don't last forever. Now is a good time for your client to evaluate his relationships. Who is important to him? How do his values reflect his choice of friends? Does each relationship enhance his sense of self and potential or suppress it? Can he permit his friend to be different? The friend doesn't have to like, believe, or be interested in everything your client does, unless he's made that an expectation for the relationship. If so, it will probably be a relationship with continual conflict.

There may be relationships that are emotionally dead but that he continues to hang onto. It is healthy to move out of destructive or stagnant relationships. As he grows, his patterns of relating will, hopefully, reflect this. Some relationships can be renegotiated; others, for various reasons, cannot. Letting go is especially important if a friendship reinforces sameness in the part of your client that he's trying to change. Pretending to be as he was because his friend can't tolerate change and won't update the relationship is destructive. If in his friend's presence he constantly feels down or insecure, he needs to check out the health of the relationship.

Saying good-bye is difficult. Usually, it's even tougher if the person is not feeling good about himself. How he tells a friend that they're in different places is the key to how the two of them deal with the grief of the loss. Sometimes just acknowledging the differentness is a good beginning. They're not in good or bad, right or wrong places—just in different ones. They should expect the emotions of loss to follow. But saying good-bye is less a blow to self-esteem if it's not put in the vein of "You've done this to me"—which, of course, is inaccurate to begin with!

Church can provide the context for people learning to relate as friends. Singles can be responsive to couples, to children, and to each other. They have much to give, and there is a great deal other members of the congregation can learn from them.

9 The Gift of Sexuality

Sexuality is part of the makeup of all human beings. It's how we look, walk, talk, dress; it's whether we're affectionate when we greet someone; it's touching a person on the shoulder. It's also the sex act, from the first eye-to-eye contact to intercourse. However, most of us limit our definition of sexuality in thinking of it only as having intercourse.

That's a rigid definition that discounts how sexual behavior relates to intimacy and responsibility. Intimacy involves exposure of our most vulnerable selves to one another. Revealing oneself to another person is full of both danger and potential. We may be rejected; yet we may be enhanced. It's sharing the hopes, the dreams, the fears, and the sacredness of life. Intimacy can but doesn't have to include the physical expression of closeness. Trust begins when we share our deepest selves with another.

I think most singles look for a theology of sexuality that applies to them. Without one, people make decisions about sex based on the momentum of feelings. But because sex is a subject that is both delicate and threatening, singles are caught between Scriptures—some of which appear contradictory when taken out of context. For example, singles are told that the Bible condones sex within marriage; yet Paul admonished Christians not to get married. Some view

Scriptures as implying that masturbation is sinful; others see it as a way to deal with sexual pressure. So people of all ages are caught between partial understanding of and little or no guidance in developing a theology of sexuality. What then occurs is that sexuality is dealt with by the person's not dealing with it; questions are asked and noncommital answers are received. Frustration gains its own momentum.

Sexuality is wrapped up in the meaning of life. It has to do with personhood. The sexual act itself is the essence of communication. The question is what you communicate—on the negative side, that a person is a sex object, a convenience, a conquest, a power trip, or a pseudocure for loneliness. Perhaps to some people a refusal of sex play means fear that the valued parts of the relationship will end. An invitation to a sexual encounter could mean trying to regain an old relationship. Perhaps we don't have emotional and intellectual intimacy with someone, so we offer sex as a substitute. Yet the realization that you are just a body to someone rather than a unique person can be devastating. Depersonalized sex has a high price tag: loss of self-esteem and the ability to trust.

Sexuality is a gift from God. However, it's a gift not acknowledged openly. I don't recall ever hearing a prayer of gratitude for the gift of sexuality! In fact, sexuality is often given "pet sin" status! We beat people over the head with verbal criticisms when we think they've misused their gift. Yet, as with other scriptural ideals, we fall short of its intended purpose. Most of us are more mature socially and intellectually than we are in our understanding and appreciation of sexuality!

Sex is not merely biology; it's personhood. Sexuality mirrors our beliefs and our values. Separate sexuality and personhood, and people are fragmented.

Sexual expression outside of marriage is not confined to non-Christians. In fact, sexual activity doesn't usually reflect the dogma of the church but rather the need of the individual. Yet many don't deal with this reality and continue to preach black/white, simplistic solutions designed to raise the guilt quotient. It's time to approach singles from where each one is rather than from where you might like them to be or think they should be. If you're going to work with singles, you must deal with the total person.

In one divorce seminar session, participants risked telling it like it is. The responses were to the question "What is it like for you as you deal with your sexuality?"

"A guy takes me out for a hamburger and expects dessert to be a night in bed. That's quite a trade-off for just a $1.95 hamburger."

"In my marriage of twenty years, our sex life was OK. I now have a well-established sex pattern, but no partner. The church says 'Don't,' and I wonder what the alternative is. My minister is married and has never been divorced. I wonder what he'd say if *he* were in my place!"

"How do you turn off the desire to be physically close when you're used to it?"

"Frankly, I hate loneliness. I know sex won't cure it, but for a little while I forget."

"I just don't let anyone at church know that this guy and I sleep together. And I have friends who do the same thing."

"I believe intercourse should be confined to marriage, but how much activity is OK prior to that time?"

"What do you do when you really don't want to sleep around? I feel too vulnerable for that. Yet since my divorce the men at work, even married ones, approach me."

"Sex was lousy in my marriage. I was accused of being frigid. Since my divorce, I've had a couple of good relationships with men. I've learned that I'm not cold and inhuman after all. And to think how long I believed it!"

"I'm a Christian, but I still have sexual needs. They didn't end with the divorce decree."

"I give out signals which apparently are interpreted as 'I'm available.' I'm not inviting sexual intimacy, but I wonder how to be friendly without being misinterpreted."

These responses were similar to ones made by the widowed. Each struggled with emotional and physical needs that were taken for granted during marriage.

You need to be aware that many enter a whirlwind of relationships during divorce or widowhood. Sometimes the concern is a developmental issue in which a person has regressed to an earlier form of behavior. It may be a developmental task that wasn't completed prior to or during marriage. The avalanche of emotions generally propels us to the stages that haven't been worked through. Other people are looking for something or trying to answer unresolved questions about themselves. Still others are trying to escape. Whatever the motive, the activity serves to express where the person is with himself and in the grief process. You may not be comfortable with this, but you can't be helpful if you don't recognize life as it is for some people.

When a person tires of the affairs, severe guilt may accompany the longing for something else. I urge you to view the person as being in a process of maturation with himself rather than reinforcing the guilt. It's useful if the person can again look at his values, discover what he accomplished or learned about himself, and focus on what he wants in the next stage of his life. Help him deal with his guilt rather than have it survive as a stumbling block to growth. It's easy to preach thou-shalt-nots; it's difficult to educate about the facts and emotions of sexuality. Living with shades of gray is facing life and people as you find them.

Sexual feelings are not reserved for those who have been married. Singles who haven't married, whether by overt choice or not, must still live with sexual feelings. During a group session composed of never-married men and women, comments such as these were voiced.

"I get so tired of being Saint Susan. I've been performing all my life—playing happy, content, and relaxed with my single status. I want a man to love me."

"I've had a few serious relationships; but after a certain point, each woman pressed for marriage. I can handle the sexual aspects, but I verbally freeze up when I think about revealing the real me. Then she'd know about my weaknesses and unresolved problems."

"I came from a small town, and the chance to meet eligible men was limited. I haven't had many opportunities to meet men that I'd even want to marry. But I still have to deal with sexual feelings."

Some people already have a theology of sexuality and are responsive to it. Others, because of age, recent single status, or lack of guidance, are in the process of dealing with themselves as sexual beings. If your client is in the latter category, this is for you.

When confused about our sexual identity, we often want others to say that our value system is OK or not OK. However, each of us must sort through and form our own values. To struggle with that process is a necessary part of adulthood. It's also an essential ingredient in starting over after a divorce or widowhood experience. If someone is manipulated into placing value judgments on others' behavior, he's fostering dependency relationships and blocking personal growth. It's far more beneficial to help someone learn to evaluate his values and make decisions which reflect them.

Following are specific areas that influence our theology of God, ourselves, and others in relation to sexuality. Examine your own feelings in relation to each one. Knowing your personal perspective is essential in understanding your potential for hearing another.

1. *Biblical vs. church positions.*—The Bible emphasizes sexuality in a positive manner. Genesis says it head-on: The man and woman were both naked and were not ashamed. Jesus in the New Testament didn't discourage this positive attitude. The church, which often isolates certain sins for preoccupation, has created the "living in sin" to relate specifically to sexuality. In so doing, many grow to believe that sex is bad and something to be ashamed of. Yet those who have sound theological concepts take seriously the positive nature of sex. Sexuality was created to be healthy, fun, and an expression of love.

However, if we're going to stress sexual ethics, let's add a large P.S. Singles receive bad publicity about the sexual issue. But if parental, social, religious, and personal values mean anything at all, let's apply them to marriage as well. How about sexual morality within marriage? I'm not necessarily referring to affairs, but rather to the emotional rape, manipulation, and exploitation that sometimes occur in the marriage bed! Some people use the marital license as a license to exploit their mate without consideration for emotional health. It's time to update views that make a person a possession of someone else.

2. *Parental values.*—The messages you received as a child influence your views of sexuality. How did your family express affection, caring, talking, touching, and so forth? Did you receive the message that sex is only for procreation and not to be enjoyed? Your parents modeled what it means, according to them, to be a man and a woman. Unless you've

had occasion to examine those subtle messages, you may not realize how much of an influence parental values are on your present attitudes.

3. *Social values.*—What are you looking for—relationships or one-night stands? Rate the following needs in terms of your priorities: physical tension release, "cure" for loneliness, friendship, way to deal with identity problems, and means to attachment.

After rating them, how do you plan to meet them? If friendship is your chief concern, you must put that ahead of cure for loneliness or ego trips. You'll have to focus energy on building relationships rather than on trying to impress people. The phenomenon of the singles bar is that it's not the place you generally go to make friends in whom you feel complete trust. You go for cruising opportunities, or, at first, curiosity. Bars provide a way to know someone without knowing him. If the experience is empty, it's because you're playing games with something not meant for game playing—intimacy.

4. *Philosophy of self.*—Who are you to yourself? You have only certain choices in relation to dealing with sexual energy. Some are consistent with biblical teachings; some are not.

    a. MARRIAGE—the ideal as set forth in Scripture.

    b. A LOVE RELATIONSHIP—built on caring, one-to-one commitment. Marriage may or may not be your goal for the relationship.

    c. ONE-NIGHT STANDS—casual sex without obligation. "Instant intimacy" does not necessarily provide the gift of understanding. Later on the result may be heightened anonymity with threads of loneliness and despair. It is mutually exploitative and designed to be temporary—but has perma-

nent consequences. Consequences of human behavior are far-reaching, and no moral decision is
isolated in its impact. Manipulation leaves its mark
on character and the ability to foster healthy relationships. If you have a variety of partners, you
opt for excluding a vital, fundamental relationship
with one partner.

d.   SUBLIMATION—using the physical tension of the
drive and channeling it into activity. It may be a
political, civic, or career emphasis. Or sexual desire
may be diverted into exercise, such as jogging,
tennis, gardening, and so forth. The emphasis is
on productively using the tension of sexual energy.

e.   MASTURBATION—a great taboo for some, but a viable option for those whose value system doesn't
create additional guilt. Masturbation can serve as
a way to release sexual energy and frustration.

The choice is up to the individual, along with the responsibility for it. With each method, your client will have to dic-
tate boundaries for himself. If he chooses the sublimation
route, he must decide how he will live within those limits.
For instance, if the person next door invites him over "to
talk" and he knows that the intent of the invitation is sexual,
then he will think ahead of time about his response. He
can choose to decline, to invite other people, or to tell his
friend what his boundaries are. People are less offended by
a remark such as "I'd rather get to know you as a person
rather than playing teasing games" than by what seems to
be rejection.

When one decides his values, limits, and expectations for
himself, then he's less vulnerable to changing mood swings.
It's a tough struggle to assume responsibility for the questions

that don't have easy answers. But each of us is called to make an integrity response—being responsible for how we understand ourselves today, knowing that tomorrow we may be at a different point in our growing maturity.

Considerations for Times with Family

10 Individuation: Families Are Designed to Disintegrate

I've been surprised by the number of people who think that they are not worth listening to, that they have nothing to offer. I've known some people who don't even listen to themselves. They verbally plow through each moment, giving double messages. Someone says yes, but the body posture says no; a woman says she's angry with a smile on her face; a man talks about feeling happy, yet his mood is that of depression.

We sometimes try to hold onto the past, not realizing that before we can meet new developmental stages, we must be able to say good-bye to old ones.

Karen was a petite, attractive woman in her thirties. She described herself as being "down." To Karen, that meant an almost immobilizing depression that had lasted over three weeks. As she rebuked herself for not "getting on top of things," tears rolled down her cheeks. Her story was not uncommon. Married for seven years. Divorced. One daughter, three years old. Karen felt pressure at work, at home, and within herself to "perform." As she told her story, she revealed that her family of origin was a very cool, calm, and collected one. Rarely did anyone display anger. In fact, when she told her mother about her current depression, she received a pep talk on how grateful she should be for the good things in life. When Karen felt anger as a child, she withdrew from everyone. There seemed to be an unwritten rule that anger was unacceptable. Now she felt herself withdrawing again. Depression, she decided, must be a bad emotion, too. At the very least, she felt that it was not tolerated in close, family relationships.

During her marriage, Karen lived out the childhood message. Since her husband had a violent temper, she assumed the role of peacemaker. The relationship didn't permit her to be angry, so her husband expressed anger for both of them! Now she was divorced. She felt angry over the pressures she experienced, but guilty for not being able to handle them. Again, the message that anger and depression were inappropriate haunted her.

The most powerful things that we've learned about ourselves and our relationships we learned as children. Each family has rules of behavior, spoken and nonspoken, that members follow. Survival, especially for a child, depends on it. However, the rules that were designed to fit certain occasions have been generalized into life rules. Unless we've had some experience that encouraged us to reevaluate, we're probably trying to fit childhood rules into adulthood. It's easy to understand why many of us feel as though our survival depends on other people. As with Karen, we follow the rules that were set for us by other people for another time of our lives.

One way that I try to discover in what ways the past is not the past is to ask someone to list the "rules" that govern his behavior. John, a man in his forties, listed forty-three rules, each designed to set himself up for feelings of guilt and failure. Some of his list included:

1. I must always be in control.
2. I should never be angry.

3. I should never argue with my elders.
4. I must always keep a smile on my face.
5. I shouldn't rock the boat.
6. I ought to be successful.
7. I should marry and have children.
8. I shouldn't trust anyone outside the family.
9. I shouldn't talk unless I have something interesting to say.
10. I should take care of other people's problems.
11. I shouldn't think of myself . . . it's selfish.
12. My opinion is always wrong.

We can discover the rules that govern our life by paying attention to all the "shoulds, oughts, nevers, and alwayses." Let's evaluate our rules. Are we adults living with childhood rules and expectations? The familiar becomes habit, and we no longer recognize it as something over which we have options. Men and women make many of the meanings they live by. If we're longing for something better, we often have to struggle against habits that are difficult to recognize. A beginning is becoming acquainted with our rules and being willing to be open to new perspectives. That requires trying new possibilities, keeping what fits our adult values and throwing out what doesn't, and practicing until the new attitudes and behavior become ours.

It's also necessary for each person to evaluate what's occurred in his life of faith. Has he lost it or renegotiated it; or is he trying to resolve the contradictions of childhood faith? That means looking past an individual minister or priest, past his mother and his father, to resolve the God issue. It's part of an identity question. All human beings have frailties and weaknesses, yet we sometimes try to place expectations of perfection on ministers. Working through the adolescent crisis requires recognizing this and growing into a mature relationship with God. So has anything new emerged from your client's childhood faith? Faith is a developmental issue. Where he was ten years ago may be different than where he is today or will be five years in the future. Life is an ongoing process of development that we never finish. Unfortunately, many don't recognize this and die spiritually and emotionally before their time.

Families are designed to disintegrate. When children reach a certain level of development, they leave their parents' home to begin their own. Parents, hopefully, learn to develop themselves so that they too are free to move into the next stage of their lives. The role of parenting is replaced with the negotiation of adult-to-adult relationships.

Individuation can be both refreshing and painful. It is especially so if a parent can't individuate from the "adult-child" or vice versa. I know one thirty-year-old man who defers all decision making until he gets his parents' advice. The parents secretly wish that he'd learn to stand on his own two feet. They don't want to hurt his feelings, yet wonder how he'll make it when they die. In all probability, each side is sending double messages and is frustrated with the other.

Individuation is a term often misunderstood. It doesn't mean turning your back on parents or children, never seeing each other, or making a geographical move. It does mean being a part of the family without giving up one's identity. Taking an "I" position with relatives means that one makes choices about his life based on his understanding of his personal values. In so doing, he's not constantly trying to maneuver to gain approval or support. Those who aren't in the process of individuation discover that they're preoccupied with how the family views their decisions. One of the classic examples is of Jan, a twenty-eight-year-old woman, who enjoys her singlehood but feels guilty about it. Her parents want her to marry, partially because that would help them to feel that they've done a good job of parenting.

During one particular seminar session, we dealt with perceived parental expectations. Obviously, how the parents understood what occurred in the family would be different. However, the focus was to begin thinking about expectations and, consequently, invisible loyalties retained about family rules or messages. As we come to understand our role in the family, we're then in a position to assume responsibility for ourself. No longer can we blame parents, God, or the world for our lives. Parents generally do the best they can, based on where *they* came from in their families of origin. Blaming parents is merely an excuse to avoid responsibility once we gain some appreciation of our parents as people. The following is how Jan understood the nonverbal rules in her family.

Counselor: "What are your perceptions of your mother's chief expectations of you during the following periods of your life?"

Teenage: "Perfection."

Twenties: "Near perfect."

Now: "More understanding."

Counselor: "What are your perceptions of your father's chief expectations of you?"

Teenage: "Rigid perfection."

Twenties: "Rigid perfection."

Now: "Rigid perfection."

Counselor: "What messages did you receive from your family about the following matters?"

1. Marriage: "Do it early so you won't get into trouble."
2. Career: "Don't work. Stay at home."
3. Myself: "Be good and everything will be OK."

4.   Success meant: "A mediocre, bland existence."

5.   Failure meant: "Disagreeing with them in what I considered important in my life."

Individuation means learning to discover our own values and not living to meet others' expectations. Whatever works for our parents in their relationship is OK for them. But as adults we must pick and choose what is ours rather than living with mythical expectations. Living not to disappoint others results in everyone feeling cheated.

I generally ask people to write a brief history of each member of their family—what qualities or traits they would attribute to father, mother, sisters, brothers, grandparents, and anyone who lived under the same roof with them as a child. I try to learn who was the "pet" child, the scapegoat, the achiever, and so forth. By observing and listening to family interaction in a new way, each person can discover what role he plays. And how he defines himself in the family emotional system is how he defines himself in the real world. That's an important realization! You can help someone working through family individuation by remembering:

1.   Individuation is a lifelong process. In times of illness, divorce, widowhood, or a major crisis, we tend to be swayed by the emotional climate in the family of origin. Especially in a divorce there is a tendency to "go home again." For extended periods of time, this can encourage regression to childhood, complete with curfews and rules. At some point a person must move out of dependency relationships and restructure life.

2.   Every family has myths, boundaries, certain taboos, and values. Learning what they are gives us leverage to retain, modify, or reject some of them. Our personal myths about families, roles, and expectations are not better than

anyone else's. They're just *ours*, and that's what makes them so powerful!

3. Families are the most powerful influence on us, regardless of how close/distant or near/far we claim to be from them. Even if parents are dead, we can keep alive the rules we learned as children. In fact, sometimes the most powerful way to stay with someone is to die! People generally conform to family rules (even as adults) or react against them. The task is to learn to take those things that *fit* you. But we can't underestimate the power we've given them.

4. When we can begin seeing parents as people rather than as authority figures, the chance for adult-to-adult relationships is born.

Family individuation is a process. You can be helpful by encouraging singles to be aware of the role they have and are playing in their family of origin. It's just as much a burden to play the favorite as it is the clown, the responsible one, or the scapegoat. How the single wants to react in the family is the question. He can refuse to play a certain role by non-verbally, without explanation, changing his role in the family.

Since people tend to "protect" members of the family of origin from real or imagined problems, it's difficult to try to renegotiate relationships. But it's important for each person to integrate his values, his words, his expressions, and his behavior. Then he is free to listen to his own internal compass rather than being boxed in by shoulds, oughts, and fears of growth. No one can mature by standing still!

11 Successfully Single: Myth or Possibility?

For most people who are not married, being single is a tremendous challenge. Even more difficult is to remain single because of the pressure to couple. Regardless of the fact that there are over 46 million singles, we live in the midst of pressure to pair. Society is not set up to encourage sampling singleness.

One thirty-eight-year-old woman revealed that her goal in life was to marry. She concentrated so much energy on pursuing a man that she didn't know what other goals she had, much less how to reach them. Her model of relating had been deference to parents, to authority figures, and to her friends in dating relationships. Consequently, whenever she wasn't in a dependency relationship, she was miserable. Since she hadn't learned to be autonomous, she hadn't even explored the potential values in her single life. Most of her years had been spent straddling the fence. She wasn't married, yet she didn't actualize singlehood. She dreamed about being part of a couple, yet postponed learning about and liking herself as a person.

Most of us talk as though we know what's going on with us, yet we have no idea. We assume that we understand ourselves and each other when we don't. This woman learned that she reacted to a message she perceived as a child: "All nice girls get married to have a man approve of them." That message became a belief and, therefore, one of her rules for living.

She'd told herself that she'd never had opportunities to marry. But as she explored her own history, she discovered choices that she'd decided not to pursue. She opted not to pick up on signals from some men, wasn't interested in others, and turned down advances for intimacy with one man. She wouldn't settle for marrying just for looks. And she realized that on occasions, she feared risking herself in an intimate relationship.

This woman grew to the point where she could give herself the option not to marry. That freed her then to consider marriage as an alternative, but not as a solution to the demands of society, parents, and friends. She had to unlearn much that she had learned in order to recognize that marriage may not be for everyone. Whether due to opportunities, goals, or interests, marriage may not suit each individual. But the single life-style is not for everyone either! And that's the whole point. Each of us must learn to look beyond myths and stereotypes to discover our own direction. Single becomes acceptable as a life-style when we become OK with ourselves.

In order to become successfully single, your client begins by owning his stereotypes for the single life. You may want to discuss one or more of these topics with him:

1.   The seventies may be permissive, but guilt about sex still endures. Most singles would not talk about their sexual relations with parents, certain friends, or some ministers for fear of disapproval. Even divorced or widowed persons are concerned about what their married children will think of them.

2.   The homosexual value system pertains to some singles,

but certainly not to all. There's a greater awareness and
sensitivity to people who are homosexual. But that doesn't
necessarily indicate an increased understanding of what homosexuality means. Dealing with homosexuality is beyond
the scope of this book, but the statement that "all unmarried
people are homosexual" is just as erroneous as is the statement that "all married people are *not* homosexual." People
marry or remain single for a variety of reasons!

3.   Many singles have not distinguished between being
lonely and being alone. To some degree everyone is living
with loneliness. It would be useful to learn to use the lonely
times as journeys inward.

4.   Being single doesn't mean that you're irresponsible,
immature, hedonistic, selfish, impotent, frigid, crazy, devoid
of personality, or a combination of these.

5.   Singles often think that they suffer isolation alone, yet
others feel the same way. Consequently, loneliness becomes
silent suffering rather than a chance for sharing with others
who are in the same place.

6.   There are fewer common denominators among singles
than most people imagine. Never-married persons have a
different understanding of the single life-style than do the
divorced or widowed. Each group, and certain ages within
each group, has a different perception of themselves and
their needs.

Walls exist when people presume to know how someone
else feels. There's no incentive to trust unless you risk knowing someone and being known. Isolation is intensified and
a sense of community lost. The single's family is made up
of those people who are significant. If there's not a sense
of community in your church, you might ask the singles
how one might be developed. They know the people and
the needs represented. Even a dialogue group to feel the

pulsebeat of those who are active in your church can be the beginning. However, the convener of such a group must have a positive attitude about singlehood. If the attempt is to parent or encourage coupling, the result is an erosion of self-esteem and trust.

Becoming aware of the advantages of singleness can be helpful in dropping the apologetic, defensive attitude about living single. When singlehood is viewed as a life-style with disadvantages and advantages, persons can deal more realistically with problems of sexuality, meeting others, going out alone, developing intimacy, dealing with loneliness, and so forth. Problems are viewed as natural, not something to feel shame over.

Another way to be helpful is to recognize that the church community includes all people. Consequently, to focus only on coupling encourages people to rush into marriage to be acceptable. Then we have the coupling, uncoupling, recoupling cycle.

Being successfully single means:

1. Having a clear value system.

2. Giving up the search for the "one and only" and devoting energy toward becoming a whole person. Marriage is an option, not a have-to.

3. Taking responsibility for your own actions.

4. Having realistic goals, working toward them, and affirming yourself.

5. Giving of yourself, your time, and your interest to volunteer projects in order to balance your capacity to give as well as receive.

6. Looking at the singles you meet as potential friends rather than as the "walking wounded."

Being successfully single is a myth or a possibility, depending on the choices we make.

12 Lives in Transition . . . **Divorce**

Divorce is a grief process. The grief that accompanies a divorce is similar to the grief process of one who's lost a mate through death. The difference is that in a divorce the corpse is still walking around. And that has all kinds of implications. When a mate dies, friends bring casseroles, condolences, and sympathy cards. In a divorce there are no casseroles and no cards, and often there is little understanding for the person.

If you have a broken relationship, you must show up for work and be efficient; your friends expect you to carry on as before; and you have to deal with the fact that most people really don't know how to be helpful. It's assumed that you had control over your life, so now you have little cause for sorrow. One man expressed it this way: "There's no way to explain what this limbo state is like. Even when people are around me, I'm alone."

This chapter is not designed to deal with causes, "rightness or wrongness," or attempt to select "guilty or innocent" parties. Rather, it offers a way to understand what occurs in the divorce process and at what points you can be helpful.

To give you an idea of the complexity of divorce, several kinds of traumas are happening at once. They may come in different orders and with varying degrees of intensity, but each one leaves an impact. There are legal, economic, parental, and friendship upheavals. The trauma of the emotional divorce and the move toward autonomy is generally very intense, and it's at this point where you might be most helpful to the divorcing couple.

One important thing to remember is that the outside composure of each party doesn't necessarily reveal how each is feeling inside. It's not uncommon for one person to appear devastated while the other one appears to cope very well, regardless of the circumstances surrounding the divorce. There could be many reasons for this. For instance, one or both people could have done much of their grieving while still in the relationship. Or sometimes a sense of euphoria exists immediately after the public announcement of divorce because of a temporary relaxation of tension. Whatever the case, the couple's emotional reaction at the time it becomes public news doesn't necessarily tell you what it's been like prior to that time; nor is it indicative of what is yet to come.

There are several experiences that one going through the emotional divorce will have. The order in which I'm listing them is only a guide. Generally, people may be in a couple of the stages at the same time or may go through one stage so quickly that you may be unaware of it. Some people begin the process in a state of shock. It's a temporary feeling, but it keeps the person from facing the grim reality all at once. A temptation would be for someone to come in and try to take over for the person. However, trying to "fix it" is not helpful because the whole purpose is to try to reorganize life without the spouse; and that can't be fixed by someone else! Sometimes this stage can be misunderstood in that the person is seen as cool and calm.

I remember one woman who thought she was doing marvelously well because she wasn't crying and wasn't depressed and lonely. This crest of enthusiasm lasted for several weeks; then she began to move into the next stage, which is typically the expression of emotion. This came at about the time she realized how painful the loss was. She interpreted this as a major setback for herself, but she was encouraged to express her grief and not to bottle it up. In so doing, she was able to move through the process rather than remaining blocked where she was. If she had been unable to work through her feelings, professional help might have been both helpful and necessary.

Attempting to cope with depression, loneliness, and even physical symptoms of distress can be overwhelming. Be available to hear the person, but don't offer advice on how all of this could have been prevented. "If only" isn't helpful! The best analogy is one using the symbolism of an automobile accident. If we meet someone who's lying on the pavement after sustaining injuries, it's not the time to offer food, water, or a conversation about how the wreck happened. It's the time to be available to the accident victim; to hear a request, if any; and to offer warmth, support, and understanding. Being present is essential!

Panic usually occurs with the gradual dawning realization of the impact of the divorce. Panic is normal and appropriate for such a stressful loss. Panic is scary, though, so it's natural to wonder, *Am I abnormal? Will I make it? Does everyone else feel this way?* Helping to allay these fears provides a support basis needed to move through to the other side of panic.

Regardless of how a divorce is decided upon, guilt feelings are a part of the process. Some people have remarked that they think they'll feel guilty forever. One man repeatedly listened on the telephone while his ex-wife lectured him on his failures. He eventually voiced his feelings of guilt and his inability to deal with them. He was encouraged to face his feelings so that he wouldn't become an emotional cripple. When he chose not to listen to the put-downs, it signaled his willingness to learn from the divorce and to begin the slow movement back into life.

Gradually, a person will move from depression into feelings of hostility. This is the time when the person is attempting to understand how and why the divorce occurred. In many relationships, the deterioration of a marriage is an orderly process, so it's important for a person to understand his role in it. Seldom is the end of a relationship totally one person's responsibility, but during the early stages of the divorce process one party usually tries to give the other full credit for the painful events. You may be helpful at the point of facilitating each person to accept how he contributed to the death of the marriage.

At some point, it may be difficult for the formerly married to return to usual activities. This could occur for many reasons. It may be because it's difficult to grieve in the presence of other people; it could be that there's not enough energy to work through feelings and keep up with the usual routine; or it may be that the person is deeply involved in reshaping his identity and trying to discover what relationships are significant. Whatever the reason, it's a time when keeping in touch is important; but pressuring the person to continue as before may increase withdrawal.

Being available through the divorce process, but not rushing in to make it "right," will help the person surrender what's dead and accept what's alive. With gradual hope, there will be a movement back into the world and the reality of the new situation. Hope will not come overnight because a divorce requires coming face to face with the unknown. To discover much in life that can be affirmed after such an experience is an enormous growth process. It's this very growth process that we must affirm; but unfortunately, it's often overlooked.

Since divorce is a reality, we must face how a minister can use his unique position to respond to those affected by it. If you're on the church staff, the first priority is to be aware of your personal feelings toward divorce. It also requires that you understand how you feel about *people* who are divorced. You may find that it's an anxiety-producing experience. Understanding the source of the anxiety and the threatening part about it will give you some leverage toward meeting people's needs.

If divorce occurs with an active couple within the church, understandably, it's likely to be more threatening to you and to your congregation. In fact, you may be asked to voice a value judgment, to ask them to resign positions of leadership, or to help decide if there's a guilty party. The important emphasis at this point is twofold. First, help the people who approach you understand and accept their own fears and feelings of loss, grief, and anxiety. In actuality, they must say good-bye to a marriage relationship and learn to relate to the individuals who were once half of a couple. Naturally, if the couple is significant to you, it's necessary that you deal with your own feelings.

Secondly, those same people will need to hear an affirmation of the scriptural ideal, while at the same time understanding that the Christian response is to meet people at their point of pain. Some persons treat divorce as an unpardonable sin. They tend to be quite vocal and critical of those who reach out to one going through a divorce. Recognize that this is not merely an intellectual response. It is an emotional one! The more threatened or insecure we are about an experience or our own marriage, the more angry we tend to become over divorce. Help these people to focus their energies on their own marriages and to do some preventive work within their marital relationship.

Some will look to you to play a parenting role, so you must know how you'd like to respond both to the divorcing couple and to those affected by it. You can be sure that whatever you have to say will at some point be repeated. And if one or both partners of the divorcing couple seek your counsel, they will in some form be asking, first, that you maintain their confidence; second, that you reassure them of your caring and of their place in the church; third, and most crucial, that you understand their pain. It's vital that one going through a divorce receive your acceptance rather than approval or disapproval, empathy rather than sympathy.

One of the ways that this can be done is through programming. Be curious about the needs of the particular singles in your church. This takes into account that there are differences in the experiences and needs of never-married singles, the widowed, and the divorced.

I've been asked, "How can a minister deal with his own feelings of failure that may result when he's been counseling a couple toward reconciliation and a divorce occurs?" This is a difficult question because many times a crisis situation is the motivation for counseling. Sometimes the desire and motivation to work on the marital relationship is present; at other times it's not. So you must determine if the counseling is in actuality the last step taken prior to divorce. If it is, it's very easy and natural to get hooked into carrying the responsibility for the marriage on your shoulders—when too much water may already be under the bridge as far as one or both of your clients is concerned. No one can give to another person the desire to work things out, any more than you could talk someone out of a depression. It's not that simple!

Be curious about the goals of the couple. One person may already be emotionally moving out of the relationship. If this is the case, your clients may be asking you to be a mediator, a referee, the funeral director for the relationship, or a facilitator to help them work with the marriage. Knowing the unvoiced expectations is a must. It's also important to get in touch with how much responsibility you feel to "save the marriage." Why would the couple feel any of the responsibility to work on the relationship if you're doing all the work? The failure of a marriage doesn't mean that you're a failure as a minister and helping agent. However, each person must struggle with the feelings of failure in his own way. The decision to divorce is not the end of your involvement; in fact, it may signal the beginning.

In a divorce everyone blames themselves and each other. The children wonder why, if parents love them, they can't love each other. Sometimes they blame themselves, wondering if they did something to cause the divorce. Parents feel guilty yet helpless against the avalanche of emotions. Each family member has a fantasy about what caused the divorce and what it would take for a reconciliation.

If would be helpful if parents and children could meet together with an objective person. When divorce has been decided upon, children should be given an explanation appropriate to their age and level of understanding. With a neutral person in the room, children can be encouraged to ask questions and learn about the new living arrangements. The parent without custody should have an adequate opportunity to define his new function in the family. Confusion over this usually results in loyalty conflict for the children. If the family can be redefined, the children have more opportunities to relate to both their father and their mother.

As you deal with generational boundaries, encourage parents to fight their battles without placing their children in the middle. When a child becomes an advocate for one parent's position over the other one, his development is impaired. This is easier said than done, but adults must be encouraged to deal with their anger or resentment in ways that don't jeopardize the children.

After the legal divorce and the restructuring of daily routines, the postdivorce phase begins. People usually describe it with remarks such as:

"I'll never trust again."

"I feel too vulnerable to take risks with people."

"When will the pain end?"

"I don't have the energy to be a good parent."

"I fill every minute so I don't have to be alone."

"How can I possibly forgive my ex?"

Eventually the grief work nears completion, and a person feels like reentering life. A frantic social life may begin; and, if not a pattern for months, this can be a good thing. It offers the opportunity to become accustomed to new dating styles, different types of people, and new interests and friends. Another stage in the growth process is reached when the frantic life-style is replaced by clear choices about activities, people, and ways to spend time. No longer is the pace an attempt to flee loneliness.

There may come a time when the first serious romantic relationship is entered. If the grief process isn't complete, the premature relationship serves to postpone its completion. Later the unresolved emotions will surface. If the relationship ends, a person will choose one of two paths: either to withdraw from taking risks in relationships or to risk love in spite of potential pain. You can be a friend during this crucial time if you can accept individuals struggling to grow. Granted, you will have to face your own issues and learn not to have all the answers. Doing so will teach you how to accept without condemnation, understand without parenting.

Friends play a complex role in the lives of those going through a divorce. On occasion you may be asked how they can be helpful. After all, friends aren't prepared to deal with divorce either. In an issue of *Home Life* magazine, I suggested some ways that friends could respond in both helpful and unhelpful ways. The don'ts are as follows:

1. Don't encourage pain by saying, "It's not all that bad." There's no way that we can make that determination about another person's life.

2. Don't accent feelings of failure by saying, "If it were me . . ." Again, you can't second-guess how you'd respond if you were faced with the same circumstances.

3. Don't use the phrase "Your kids will suffer." That's one area in which a great pain and struggling has already occurred and will continue to play a part in the process. The parents are well aware of the effects the divorce has on children.

4. Don't ask how the person can still come to church or verbally beat him over the head with Scripture quotations. If you're going to quote Scripture, tell of the new hope, new beginnings, and forgiveness available.

5. Don't try to decide who's to blame. There are no innocent parties; and regardless of how much of the history of the relationship you're aware of, the fact is that you didn't *live* in the marriage.

6. Don't take it upon yourself to decide when the person is ready for an active social life.

7. Don't ask for explanations. You'll be told what the person wants you to know.

8. Don't plan holidays to include both of the divorcing couple. It's no longer as it was; invite one but not both on the same holiday.

9. Don't pass on tidbits of gossip.

10. If you take sides—and the divorcing couple always knows if this has been done and whose side—then understand that one relationship may end. Perhaps it can be renegotiated later, but there's an excellent chance that it won't.

Following is a list of positive responses:

1. Respond with genuineness. If you don't know the words, you can with integrity say, "I don't know what to say, but I care."

2. Call at the spur of the moment to invite your friend out to dinner. That can be one of those serendipity experiences.

3. Offer to baby-sit so that the custodial parent can go out for the day or in the evening.

4. Allow the person to withdraw, talk, or be silent when he needs to.

5. Be sensitive to time and place. Crowds and work situations are not the best times to inquire about the divorce, feelings, arrangements, and so forth. You may be putting the person on the spot at a time when he is trying to keep emotions under control.

6. Be as natural as possible, and allow the person to handle his own life.

7. Think of the divorce as a death experience. We tend to be more patient with the person when we understand his emotions.

8. Realistically build up self-esteem.

9. Ask your friend if there's anything that you can do for him, but be prepared to accept that sometimes there will be nothing.

10. Understand that economics must play a part in a changing life-style. So if you're inviting someone as a guest, let that be known at the time of the invitation.

Divorce is a time of endings and beginnings. How people respond makes a difference. To meet someone where he is is an encouragement to pick up the pieces and live on. Is that not the message of the God of "the second chance"?

13 Lives in Transition . . . **Widowhood**

"When I heard the words that pronounced the death of my loved one, the unexpected shock was staggering. There was a strong feeling of unreality: It must be a mistake. But the tightness in my chest and the pounding of my head reminded me of its truth. I closed my eyes to escape the pain, but memories haunted the darkness. I breathed deeply for control, but each breath tingled my burning lungs. The air seemed colder; the days were longer; the nights felt endless. Yet I must go on and on . . ."

Those were the words written by one who'd felt death touch a loved one. Our lives are filled with good-byes. Even the little losses are worthy of our grief. For we must say good-bye to events, years, circumstances, pets, and people as we begin new stages of our lives. When a mate dies, we sometimes weep because we are still living. The struggle is demanding.

The stages of the grief process are similar to those of a person experiencing a divorce, but there are dissimilarities. With death, there may be a certain nobility that's not in divorce. In fact, some choose to wear "widow/widower" as a badge for the rest of their lives. Others try to reorganize life, meet new people, and live toward the future rather than in the past. Either way, it's a painful experience. Those who are divorced may secretly wish their ex-spouse had died because society would be more understanding. With death we have a ritual to follow. Friends know how to be responsive.

After the death of a mate, the "Why?" question haunts sleepless nights. The living partner physically aches, reaches out to the now-empty pillow, and wonders, *Can I make it?* His life has changed, whether or not he recognizes it in the first fogging shock. But the aftermath passes, and he's forcibly aware that his life is moving on. In his darkest hours he may contemplate suicide; but somehow the life drive moves him into tomorrow.

There will be friends, well-intentioned as well as curious, who will prematurely say to him, "How well you've gotten over it." Just because he doesn't bleed openly is no signal of the grief's conclusion. Perhaps he now realizes that people don't want to meet sadness every time they talk with him. He alone carries his loss.

Some friends will ask when he plans to date or remarry. Perhaps they can't imagine anyone choosing to be alone; or perhaps they'd feel more secure in their own marriage if he were safely married! However, he doesn't have the desire or the energy to meet other people's expectations.

Mourning takes time. There's no time schedule, no successful way to move through it. He can call forth all of the inner resources he can muster and sometimes is answered by a hollow pit in his stomach. The deepest despair is often the beginning of less pain and more bearable anguish.

Grief has many forms. He may be calm on the outside and jelly on the inside. He may react to insomnia with pills, overeat, or withdraw from food entirely. He knows deep inside that if he doesn't take care of himself and begin to see people, he'll slowly wither away. And he wonders, *Is that a wish or a warning?*

Grief turned into depression for long periods of time can be destructive. He thinks of Job and believes he understands Job better than before. He remembers to remember that Christians aren't immune to grief or problems. What a painful awareness when on his knees he has his first angry, crying conversation with God. God hears him, but he wonders if God's listening. He repeats his pleas again to make certain. He recalls a sign he'd seen, "Faith means not to quit." But he questions, *How long can I go on with the pain?*

There are ways that you can be helpful to someone who has lost a mate through death. The grief process differs in terms of the meaning it has for each person. Often this is related to how the mate died. Both widows and widowers grieve, although our culture has encouraged women to be more expressive about it. There are no age, color, sex, or race boundaries when a person most needs support. Yet when we need help most is generally when we're least able to request it. Six weeks after the funeral, holidays, anniversaries, long evenings, and weekends are times when initiative by other people is important. If you try to be supportive in offering help and discover that the answer is no, be careful not to interpret it as rejection. It may mean "I'm not ready." It takes time to want to be with people or join activities again. The widow/widower has an internal time clock that requires our sensitivity. The following may offer handles to begin a ministry of this kind:

1.   Do not force bereaved persons into new relationships by encouraging removal of the wedding band. Each will do it when ready to say good-bye to the mate and former marital security.

2.   Be sensitive to the person who has retreated into seclusion. It's a big temptation to withdraw forever, but at some point the effort will be made to reenter life. He can't find purpose and meaning with people if he lives behind closed doors.

3.   Although most widow/widowers are past age forty, "being old" is a decision we make through self-contempt and premature helplessness. Help a person use the lonely times to reassess strengths, values, and interests.

4.   The widowed may choose to remain in their coupled world of friends. Encourage them to expand their involvements in the community, make additional friends, travel, and visit relatives and children. In dealing with long-standing relationships with friends and children, work to renegotiate the relationships based on a positive identity rather than giving the person an easy out for becoming overly dependent on others. This is to be done when a person is ready to reenter life. It's not meant as a way to try to escape the grief process.

5.   Help the person look at his options and choices and not settle into an emotional rut. Help him learn how to be with people without constantly trying to change them or wearing a "W" to signal personal helplessness. A good rule is to do for people what they can't do for themselves, and not to do what they can do or learn to do. Timing and an understanding of the stages of grief are essential here!

6.   Talk openly about the deceased spouse. Share anecdotes with the widowed person, and encourage friends to do the same. Doing so helps the person know of others' loss, reinforces that it's acceptable to grieve, and encourages movement through the recovery process.

7.   Help the person feel more comfortable with singleness by aiding him in learning to be autonomous. Don't treat

anyone as half a person or encourage false "completeness" by urging him to rush into marriage.

8.   Aid the person in talking about the death with his children. They grieve as well, but too often a silent wall is erected so as not to upset anyone. Phrases such as "sleeping," "passed away," and so on convey less than a finality about the death. It's important for children to learn about the natural events of birth and death and to grieve without guilt.

9.   The widowed person must learn to live with himself, his family, and the rest of the world. No one lives in a vacuum.

10.   When the person is ready to make changes in the arrangement of the furniture, encourage it. There may be some initial guilt and a feeling of betraying the former mate. Help in the understanding that learning to live as a single is no reflection on the former marriage.

11.   There may be unexpected sexual advances for which the person is unprepared. These may come from friends, strangers, in-laws, or the husband or wife of a best friend. Although the invitation may prompt feelings of guilt, the widowed person must learn to recognize that people act out their fantasies when they perceive someone as being vulnerable. The person will have to decide how to respond to the "sexual volunteers."

12.   Encourage an exercise program, financial planning, social participation, goal setting, and so forth, perhaps by offering such a program in your church.

13.   Help the person move from self-pity to doing things for other people. Recovery means looking beyond oneself.

14.   Remember that the way a person dies affects how survivors go through the grief process. In the case of suicide or in any sudden death, the person left is dazed, shocked. He goes through the motions of the funeral, but slowly the

full impact hits. There are periods of trying to recapture the mate, listening for the loved one's voice, and refusing to believe the death. Emotional sobbing, anger, and depression accompany the loss of the loved one and his meaning. Acceptance of widowhood means giving up the role and identity as husband or wife. Several weeks after the death, it would be helpful for the person to be able to ask any questions about the events that occurred during the time of shock.

In the event of suicide, there is not only guilt, but shame as well. It's agonizingly difficult to acknowledge that one's mate took his own life. There's a "guilt by association" effect which sets the person apart, even from other widowed persons. He must be helped to gain a new perspective on life, feelings, ideas, and future plans. This usually occurs within the context of a counseling situation, so that structure as well as a relationship of trust are formed. Once the person can more freely talk about suicide in public, he is freer from the self-imposed stigma.

In the case of the terminally ill patient, the preparatory grief begins with diagnosis. Elisabeth Kübler-Ross has written several books that are useful if you want an in-depth look at the process of death and dying. Terminal illness provides the patient and family with an opportunity to complete unfinished business with each other. However, the longer the terminal illness, the less time the survivors may have spent doing things important in their own lives. Relationships may have been neglected; physical health may be affected. It would be helpful if you could spend time with the survivors on these kinds of concerns.

Death gives meaning to life. If we could live forever, time would have no importance. If we could do everything over, it wouldn't matter how we did things. Because time is finite, it is valuable. The knowledge of our own mortality not only gives life meaning, but also can motivate us to live well the time we do have.

14 Lives in Transition . . . **Single-parent Families**

I once asked a group of one-parent families if there was anything good about the divorce they'd experienced. The room was full of parents, all ages, male and female, those with custody, those without. Their answers were quite revealing because they didn't negate the pain of the divorce, but they had a perspective that's often overlooked.

One man volunteered that at least the emotional fog was cleared away. His son had felt guilty about the fighting between his parents. He thought that he'd caused it—a feeling that was unknown to his parents until the family began dealing with divorce issues.

Another woman explained that at least the divorce was an honest, out-in-the-open admission that they couldn't get along. Always before, they'd tried to pretend affection. The children picked up the nonverbal vibrations of unresolved anger. But they had no way to check out their perception since the parents tried to cover up by pretending that they were getting along.

Divorce is painful. Ideally, an intact family is the healthiest form, but only if the parents have a healthy, nondestructive marriage.

Not all one-parent families result from divorce. The death of a spouse, separation due to military careers, institutional confinement, desertion, or career traveling may create one-parent families. Unwed mothers often retain child custody. Increasingly, single adults are permitted to adopt a child. To be responsive, you must understand who the one-parent families are and how available, if at all, the other parent is.

Ideally, the church community can be an emotional and physical support base. This can best be done in a congregation which has redefined the meaning of family. In our society, the "traditional" family of husband, wife, and children is not the only family type. It's a subtle blow to self-esteem to hear Sunday after Sunday a reference to "family activities" that exclude one-parent families. A sensitive minister can encourage the healthy development of children and adults in one-parent families by broadening the definition of family. This can easily be reflected in church announcements, programming, and even in sermon anecdotes. It's time to recognize and be sensitive to families as people live within them. For instance, you can emphasize good parenting skills as they relate to both traditional and one-parent households. The "One-parent Family Guidelines" are aimed at single parents but should prove helpful to counselors as well.

1. As a parent, you must take care of yourself well in order to have the energy to be a responsive parent.

2. Explain the new realities of family life to your children, being careful that they don't assume guilt over their occurrences.

3. Children may share home responsibilities appropriate to their age and development. Don't make emotional demands that are not theirs to share; they're not spouse replacements.

4. Discipline for behavior rather than for the feelings and thoughts of the child.

5. Study the needs of children in particular stages of their lives so that you can appropriately respond to developmental issues.

6. Don't try to be both parents. You're the mother or the father, but not both. Even if one parent chooses not to visit, you can honestly respond that you don't understand why that's the way it is. Making the other parent either a devil or a saint sets your child up for disappointments. You can't promise love or goodness in order to protect a child. Doing so will only result in your not being trusted when your child is old enough to make his own judgments. Allow children to form their own opinions and relationships with each parent.

7. Quality and quantity time are important with children. Explain the reality of your new job or training responsibilities to your child rather than feeling guilty over the changes that a new life-style has demanded.

8. Don't make your child a spy, mediator, or little adult. Children sometimes misrepresent episodes between you and your former mate and will play you against each other. Parents who divorce are divorcing each other, not the children.

9. Children learn roles by watching other models. Church members, neighbors, teachers, friends, and relatives can serve this function.

10. Give the child the freedom to develop relationships with grandparents, if possible. By doing so, you're encouraging your child to learn to value people for who they are. You permit your child to learn from people in the last period of their lives. Keeping grandparents out of the picture sometimes is an expression of unresolved dependency ties that you have with your parents.

11. Remember that growing up is a stormy period, and all of a child's problems are not related to death or divorce

experiences. If you treat children as people, not as possessions, you realize that they too are sensitive to events and people around them.

12.   Mothers (or fathers) with child custody frequently become "super moms." They spend most of their time parenting and sacrifice their own personal growth in the process. This has the opposite effect from the one intended. Children feel overly responsible for parents, while parents feel guilty for trying to grow socially and intellectually.

When dating begins the children often cry, and parents give in to the pressure. The socialization process is then postponed. Their tears may be asking, "Are you going to leave me? Will you come back?" Responding to these cues can help the parent to clarify the parent/children relationship and to reaffirm his love for them.

If your client is a mother or father without custody, he may feel a deep longing for times with his children. If, in the case of divorce, he has visitation rights, it's important for him to put time and energy into being with his children. He's their biological parent; being the psychological parent is a process that continues beyond birth. He should forego the temptation to make visitation weekends exclusively party time. His children need the privileges of getting to know him and how he lives and of participating in the routine of his life. He may not have quantity time, but he can make quality count.

The single parent especially should pay attention to his children and their feelings. He's a role model. How he disciplines, the morality he exposes them to, how he relates to his faith—all are taught during this period. When one grows and learns about his children at every age, he promotes their health as well as his relationship with them.

As one who relates to single-parent families within the

church, you can be helpful by sponsoring groups for junior and senior high school children. They have many common feelings and questions about their life-styles. Rap sessions can be productive in getting questions, misconceptions, and anger out in the open. Permitting them to share their concerns with a group of peers and with you can be very healing.

With parents, you can set up courses on finances, auto repair, forming healthy relationships, dealing with guilt, parent-child relationships, and a multitude of other topics. You can organize mother's-day-out programs, baby-sitting services, and small support groups. The church can be the healing community that meets people where they are and tries to help them deal with life as it is.

15 Turning Points . . . **Getting Ready for Marriage**

Most couples view premarital counseling as the ritual included with bridal showers, planning the wedding, and selecting china. We take seriously the preparation for college, careers, and even our leisuretime activities. Yet the most intimate of relationships is begun in a cloud of ignorant bliss! We have no idea of the demands that we place on marriage and of what the marriage demands of us. Although it would require another whole book to even begin to adequately deal with premarital issues, I would be remiss not to mention it here.

If you provide a premarital emphasis, consider the following phases: (1) Have a series of three to six sessions with a couple prior to marriage. If time or training won't permit that, develop a referral source for that purpose; and (2) contract with the couple to see them within one year after their marriage for at least a weekend retreat. The purpose would be to work with the relationship *after* the honeymoon is over and, hopefully, before unhealthy patterns are established in emotional concrete. Such an emphasis creates a preventive approach to problems. It also states that your church is committed to the fact that healthy marriages require hard work. They don't just evolve through good intentions.

In premarital sessions, you can discover the couple's expectations for the marriage. Naturally, they would probably expect more than the relationship could possibly deliver. The wedding vow provides an image, although an unrealistic one, of a marital relationship; but it offers no how-to in terms of achieving it. Before marriage is the time to plant the seeds that the marriage will change and grow. The couple won't understand the meaning of your words until the relationship begins to mature. During the first growing pains, they may remember your message—flexibility and change make up the essence of a good marriage.

Marriage is not an event, but a process of self and relationship discovery. However, most of us worship an image of marriage as set by tradition, parents, friends, or our mate. The image is even more unrealistic because any unresolved issues we have are taken into the marriage. If we make marriage an emotional finishing school, we can continue maturing in individuation, intimacy, sexuality, and roles. If the relationship prevents growth, it eventually reacts to the stress.

Premarital counseling tends to be high-anxiety counseling because it's perceived as a threat to the relationship. And often the more troubled the premarital relationship, the less likely that counseling will help. Following is a general outline of what people need to consider prior to marriage.

1. How was it for each person growing up?
    a. Messages received in the family of origin.
    b. Have each person talk about his future in-laws— how they show affection, how they fight, who plays what role, and so forth. Check to see how that fits with the perceptions of the one who lived in the family.
    c. Dating experiences until they met each other—

how the relationships ended, whether each has
had experience forming relationships, and so on.

2. The meaning of life around general issues.
   a. Where each person is going in life and what plans
      he has for getting there.
   b. Religion—affiliation, meaning, attendance as a
      couple.
   c. Professional or career interest—how decided, one
      or both working after marriage, how decisions are
      made about moving to other cities.
   d. Social network—couples as well as individual
      friends. Marital relationships can become stagnant
      if the primary relationship excludes friendships.
   e. Interests—books, hobbies, records, and so forth.

3. Coupling relationship.
   a. How they met each other, where, doing what,
      what attracted each.
   b. Details of why they fell in love.
   c. How they decided to marry each other.
   d. What kind of man she perceives him as being,
      and vice versa. (You're testing for the reality of
      their perception of each other. Is there freedom
      to be different from each other?)
   e. Relationship to in-laws—where will they spend the
      first Christmas as a married couple? How will it
      be decided? How was it decided by what name
      each would call the future mother and father-in-
      law? (You're trying to determine the degree of
      individuation.)

4. Intimate life.
   a. Before each other; with each other.
   b. Who does what to whom? Who is the aggressor?
   c. How anger and affection can be expressed.

5. Projection of five years from now.
   a. Where they might be living.
   b. Environment.
   c. Career(s).
   d. Marriage.
   e. Children.
   f. Imagined problems that will be confronted.

In each instance, you're looking for *how* the couple works through the situation rather than an actual problem resolution. Provide the couple with feedback as to what you think you're hearing. If they explain it all away rather than being curious about it, they don't want to see it. Hear their statements without becoming defensive or aggressive. If the relationship has problems, they may return for help. And if they agree to attend a retreat to update their relationship, that's even better. People are unpredictable. Those relationships that you think won't make it sometimes survive anyway! The essence of premarital counseling is to encourage both flexibility and the willingness to shed behavioral patterns that no longer fit the maturity of the relationship.

For Further Study

Bach, George R., and Wyden, Peter. *Intimate Enemy.* New York: William Morrow and Company, 1969.

McGinnis, Tom. *Your First Year of Marriage.* New York: Doubleday Company, 1976.

Mace, David. *Getting Ready for Marriage.* Nashville: Abingdon Press, 1972.

16 Turning Points . . . **Remarriage**

Remarriage after divorce or widowhood has become an increasing phenomenon. If first-time partners are unprepared for married life, the individuals (and their children) who remarry are heir to a unique set of problems. Preparatory work with couples and their families is essential to promote health in those relationships.

The focus of this chapter is not the rightness or wrongness of remarriage. Rather, the purpose is to offer some insight into the problems and challenges that face individuals who remarry.

At present, there is more research available on the *stability* of second marriages than on the quality of the marriages. Of course, marital stability and success, in the sense of serving the needs of the mates, are not the same things. More research is necessary both in the areas of divorce and widowhood.

What is evident is that there are problems specific to remarriage, and greater emphasis is needed in preparation for these roles. Briefly, the complexities arise because through the former marriage there are considerations with children, financial and custodial settlements, former in-laws, the former social life, and potential doubling of parental roles.

The extent to which a person has worked through the end of the former marriage has an impact on the remarriage. Naturally, unresolved emotional and legal aspects are carried into the new relationship.

If the parent is living, most children retain some form of relationship. If the parent is dead, the child may form a bigger-than-life, glorified series of memories about him. It's especially important that children work through the grief of the loss and not feel that a new parent figure is a replacement of a mother or father.

Because of the ties associated with the former marriage, such as finances, previous in-laws, friends, and other relatives, together with the roles, functions, and relationships of the new marriage, there can be great ambiguity and role overload. If you drew a family tree in such a situation, represented might be four parent figures, eight grandparent figures, siblings, step-siblings, half-siblings, and little or no definition of the roles and responsibilities of each.

In second marriages, children and financial problems are among those listed as major difficulties. Will children call the new parent figure "Mother" or by her first name? How will the child introduce the stepmother to friends? The new mate can't possibly respond to his stepchildren as he would his own—at least not for a period of time. Yet sometimes it's expected that he do so. And if the mother has formed intense dependency relationships with her children, it is more difficult for the husband to enter the family as a full member.

If the father remarries, he often feels awkward visiting with his children regardless of the place or times of the visits. Feelings of embarrassment over the remarriage often are both part of his and his children's reactions. So a man may feel caught between the demands and lack of definition of the two families. His complaint may be voiced by the reaction that financial assistance is the only contribution he makes. If he doesn't hear from family members except when money or services are wanted, that tends to increase the resentment.

Tensions also rise over the emotional upheavals that can occur in second marriages. If children haven't adjusted, then the marriage is affected. Even decisions such as whose house to live in can create anxieties and invisible loyalties. If one has lived alone for a period of time, he's accustomed to his schedule, eating habits, bedtime routines, and so forth. Tension between loyalty to biological children and the desire to please one's marriage partner add to the conflicting emotions.

With such ever-present problems, preparation for remarriage is a must. People tend to marry the same type of person as their first mate if they haven't worked through the first marriage. Old patterns of behavior are reconstructed in the new marriage, and partners react to each other as they did to their former spouse. Some couples go to the other extreme and refuse to deal with differences between them. They feel too battle-scarred to deal with important issues that will involve anger, so they do the worst possible thing— nothing!

Remarriages are potentially productive and healthy if couples have worked through their former relationships and have set boundaries and new roles for themselves in the new one. The couple will greatly enhance their preparedness for any emotional upheavals if they look at potential problems *before* the actual marriage. Have the couple, and later the children, talk about appropriate new living arrangements. Following are areas important to discuss prior to marriage.

1. Express the financial, legal, custody, and visitation privileges of the first marriage. Discuss feelings about the first marriage. If it ended by death, how did the person die; what were the circumstances; how does the person contemplating remarriage view the relationship now?

2. Relate feelings about relationship with ex-spouse and in-laws.

3. Discuss feelings about visitation arrangements.

4. Express feelings about financial arrangements.

5. Exchange views on parenting.

6. Discuss traditional marriage (use outline that applies in chapter 15) issues.

7. Talk about possibilities for remarriage adjustment.

   a. Define role between children and new spouse (what name called, discipline, responsibility, and so forth).

   b. Define role between parent's new spouse and children.

   c. Define role between new in-laws and children's grandparents of former marriage.

   d. Relate expectations for household management.

   e. Define role as husband, wife, man, and woman.

8. Talk about responsibilities of each partner to children in areas of finances and discipline.

9. Discuss how the second marriage will be different from the first—expectations, goals, meaning of relationship to couple.

10. Express how each person will deal with "instant" family as well as achieve time as a couple.

11. Relate how each plans to promote individual growth as well as relationship and family growth.

12. Discuss how faith and church are involved in families—how decisions will be made as to importance, which church to attend, and so on.

Considerations for the Counselor

17 For Ministers Only: You Can't Lead from a Position Behind

Occasionally you may be tempted to label a person by a symptom. Single adult is a role filled by countless people. It is not a pigeonhole to dehumanize people. Hopefully, your attempt to understand human behavior will not lead you to make final definitions about individuals you meet. If you do classify people according to experiences they've had, hopefully you're interested in how those judgments will help you as well as why you make them. Classifications are arbitrary, rigid, and sometimes merely intellectual snobbishness. It is with that understanding that you can deal with this paradox: We must not minimize a person's potential for change and growth; yet we must recognize that improvement means facing who he is and learning to become who he can be.

An understanding of the extremes of behavior is necessary for your own comfort. But you may learn that the strength to be helpful comes in being curious about how a person has experienced his life rather than in judging it good or bad, right or wrong, normal or abnormal. If you can use generalizations to begin to understand, but then promptly give up your pigeonhole labels, you can be a facilitator of growth. Meet people where they are rather than offering a pronouncement of where they should be.

As I've mentioned, you can't lead someone any further in personal growth than you've gone yourself. You may be able to explore with someone, but not from a position behind him. So here are the warnings as you approach the guideposts of the journey.

If you're working with an individual in counseling, you will become enormously important to that person. (When working with couples and families, the counselor is not as personally significant.) That relationship is where he will try out manipulation, joy, sadness, anger, guilt, and new behavior. At some point you will reach an impasse, and that's where significant growth can occur. If you are not trained in counseling; if your boundaries are not set; if your own homelife is disintegrating; and if when needed you're not in a supervisory or counseling process, watch out. You have the potential to be seduced by strong emotions! The violation of the trust of the client is inappropriate. Perhaps there's no one more susceptible to this than a minister who is called on by his church to fill all roles.

If you're not trained to do long-term counseling, you must deal with the question of what's in the best interest of your client. Pressure to fill roles you're not trained to fill is an issue which, sooner or later, you'll have to face. Assess your strengths and how you can best serve God and be responsive in your ministry. Either receive professional training if you're going to do counseling, or learn how, when, and to whom you'll refer people.

There are those who'll read this chapter and be offended at the suggestion that ministers could have an affair with a church member. Deal with your anger that, alas, ministers are human too! But recognize that it has occurred. The best safeguards are training, boundaries, and a healthy family life. If there's stress in your personal life, seek your own guide for healthy recovery.

Before I deal with referrals, I must make one footnote. The mental health community is probably neither as good nor as bad as it is often labeled. There are competent professionals as well as marginal ones. All types of value systems, expertise, and training are represented. Consequently, it is important that you refer to competent professionals who work within a Christian perspective.

You will have to discover who the experienced professionals are in your community and what their areas of specialization are. You can't take someone's ethical competence for granted just because they hold themselves out to the public as a counselor or therapist. Some communities have no one qualified; others contain so many that making a choice between them is a problem. Following are general guidelines to help you make those judgments:

1.   Become aware of the difference in training, degrees, and supervision that are part of mental-health workers. You may have social workers, clinical psychologists, marriage and family therapists, and psychiatrists in your community. In some states a person can call himself a marriage counselor, yet have no formal training in the field.

2.   Realize that if you refer couples, even those contemplating divorce, it's important to know whether the professional has an individual or marital approach. It's more helpful to the relationship when the professional is willing to see the couple or the family members during the same session. Only then can all aspects of the marriage or family be seen. If the professional has an individual frame of reference, he will insist on only seeing one person at a time, usually the "identified patient." Not only is valuable information missed, but routinely seeing a couple individually for what is a relationship problem may serve to escalate a separation.

3.   The graduate degree itself is not the issue as much as is ethical competence. The day of the general practitioner

in counseling will soon be over. A marriage counselor, for instance, cannot be expected to be equally competent in dealing with divorce, adolescents, sexual problems, financial concerns, or career counseling. Determine the areas of specialization and refer appropriately.

4. Some states have licensing qualifications; others do not. If you can't find a local listing of qualified professionals, you can write to one of the following organizations for information of those in your vicinity.

American Association of Marriage and Family Counselors, 225 Yale Avenue, Claremont, California 91711. AAMFC is the certification organization for marriage and family counselors. It requires a minimum degree and number of supervisory hours to become a clinical member.

American Psychological Association, 1200 Seventeenth Street, N.W., Washington, D.C. 20036. Most professionals in this organization are experimental and research-oriented. Determine those interested in and trained for working in a therapy setting.

National Council of Family Relations, 1219 University Avenue, S.E., Minneapolis, Minn. 55414. This is an interest group to which many professionals belong.

American Psychiatric Association, 1700 Eighteenth Street, N.W., Washington, D.C. 20009. This organization determines the level of training of its members. Just as with the American Psychological Association, most training is in working with individuals. You will have to determine whether the psychiatrist has had additional work with couples or families.

American Association of Social Workers, 1535 H Street, Suite 600, Washington, D.C. 20005. This organization is one of the largest and has many marriage, family, and divorce counselors as members.

American Association of Pastoral Counselors, 3 West 29th Street, New York, New York 10001. The training specializes in intense work with people. Many members are also in some of the previously listed organizations.

5.   Talk with those who appear to be professionally competent. Ask those questions which are important to you, and inquire about the process of referral. Realize that all clients will not work well with all therapists. But that doesn't mean that the client can't be helped in another professional relationship.

Ministers, unfortunately, have more than their share of expectations placed on them. People will reveal the most intimate details of their lives to you and then retreat, wishing they hadn't said so much. They'll worry about whether you told the church staff or if you'll use their story in a sermon example; and sometimes they will withdraw from the church community so as not to face you. So part of your task, if you're choosing not to be involved in process counseling, is learning not to glean any more information than necessary to make an appropriate referral. Compassion for pain doesn't necessarily require knowledge of all the details!

It does mean that in the first interview you want to learn the nature of the problem and how the person has handled it so far. At that point you can formulate what can be done about it. You might contract to see the person for a certain number of weeks, or you might choose to refer him. With issues such as a divorce or widowhood, identity questions, or depression, counseling on a periodic basis may not be sufficient. The sooner the person can enter a consistent therapeutic process, the more readily he will work through the problems.

If you don't have the time, interest, training, or energy to be involved as a counselor, you still have the most important function of minister and friend. In those roles, you can offer a much-needed support system that can parallel the counseling process.

There may be times when you feel that you can be the primary counselor to the person, but are ambivalent as to whether you choose to. Listen to your gut feelings and learn their message. Perhaps the following questions can aid in understanding your mixed reactions:

1. Can you avoid taking sides, as in the case of a couple pursuing a divorce?

2. Do you feel the need to rush in with a solution to the problem as a way to deal with your anxiety? Or can you work to clarify what the issues are?

3. Is your role clearly defined? Does your client think of you as minister, judge, mediator, answer giver, or counselor?

4. Does your manner encourage discussion of the problem without dumping?

5. Are you pursuing a personal interest that may have little or nothing to do with the person's presenting problem?

6. How personally involved are you with the person, the person's family, or the issue involved?

7. Can you tolerate a strong emotional climate within the room?

8. Are you learning about other significant relationships in the person's life?

9. Do the church staff, deacons, or members have expectations about how such problems are resolved?

10. Are you under pressure from the person or other church members to be involved in a counseling process, even if it's against your own judgment?

If your answers reveal that you're too close to the situation or the people, regardless of the reason, a referral might be in the best interest of the single adult. Distance often provides the ability to talk about that which is painful.

When you do choose to work with a person beyond the first interview, it's important to be clear about how often you'll have sessions, within what time frame, and what expectations your client has both for the sessions and the changes he wants to make.

From the time a person first calls you, the whole point is termination. At some point he will have done the work he wants to do and it's time to say good-bye. Moving toward that final session is accomplished when you talk about what growth has occurred and what changes he's working through. Aid him in claiming his growth, while at the same time letting him know he can call if he wants to do more work later on. Often the last session is like a carnival—laughter, jokes about what used to be a painful issue, curiosity about whether he could call later, gratitude for your involvement. Termination also involves anger, for good-bye is difficult. People will deal with the anger based on how effectively they've been able to say good-bye in other relationships.

Obviously, in some instances, people will end counseling before you feel they're ready. You can't pressure someone into remaining longer than he wants to, but you can help him clarify how he made the decision to stop the process. Once it's clarified and the decision is made to terminate, you acknowledge and affirm the client's responsibility for making his own decisions and leave the option open for reentering counseling at another time. The client may know better than anyone the rhythms that affect his life. It's a privilege to have been a part of his journey. For we are both teachers and learners.

THE ENDING AND BEGINNING

Epilogue

Today I completed this manuscript. After living with it for months, it's time to say good-bye and move on. Endings and beginnings are accented during the Christmas season. It's a time of hope and celebration; but it's also a remembrance of times past. Each of us has people and experiences that make memories; some of them are painful ones. But each of us reflects on the family of man and how we're involved in it.

The birth of Jesus made truth personal. So his birthday is very much a celebration of relationships. For people who are lonely, afraid, or living their first Christmas alone, it can be a season of sadness. Singles are well aware of the obstacle course called holidays.

As you hear people where they are, be aware that your words can kill or bring life, depending on how you use them. As you reach for something beyond yourself, remember the paradox:

"He that findeth his life shall lose it: and he that loseth his life for my sake shall find it" (Matt. 10:39).

NANCY POTTS

Christmas Eve 1977

Singlespeak

During the Sunday School hour in three Houston Baptist churches, single adults responded to a confidential information sheet. They were asked to state candidly their impressions about the following statements:

1. I come to church looking for . . .
2. What I would most like ministers and church leaders to understand about being single (or the single life-style) is . . .
3. The main disadvantage, or most difficult part, of being single is . . .
4. The biggest advantage of being single is . . .

Following are unedited, representative responses from those who completed the forms. Singles from South Main Baptist Church, First Baptist Church, and Tallowood Baptist Church participated as a way to give you added insight into their worlds.

1. I come to church looking for . . .

(Female respondents, ages eighteen to thirty-five)

"Bible study and fellowship." (Never married, age twenty-eight.)

"An opportunity to meet other Christians my age." (Divorced, age twenty-five.)

"Encouragement and support in my spiritual growth." (Never married, age twenty-four.)

"A close fellowship with other single adults." (Never married, age twenty-four.)

"Fellowship with others who are like myself—searching for something more to life than work and parties with no purpose or substance." (Never married, age twenty-four.)

"A place of service." (Never married, age twenty-four.)

"Meeting people in search of a better life with Christian goals." (Divorced, age thirty-three.)

"Fellowship—both Christian and social." (Never married, age thirty.)

"Something to fill the empty gap in my life." (Divorced, age twenty-nine.)

"Fellowship and a support system." (Separated, age thirty-three.)

"The Lord's help in my life." (Divorced, age twenty-five.)

(Male respondents, ages eighteen to thirty-five)

"Fellowship." (Never married, age thirty-four.)

"A sense of community and support." (Never married, age twenty-eight.)

"Bible teaching and fellowship with other Christians." (Never married, age twenty-three.)

"To find a marriage partner." (Never married, age twenty-seven.)

"Nice girls." (Never married, age twenty-five.)

"Other Christian singles." (Never married, age twenty-one.)

"Fellowship and a marriage partner." (Never married, age twenty-seven.)

"Strength." (Divorced, age thirty-five.)

"Inspiration and social contact." (Never married, age twenty-eight.)

"Hope and encouragement." (Never married, age twenty-six.)

"A chance to serve God in a fulfilling way." (Never married, age twenty-four.)

(Female respondents, ages thirty-five to fifty)

"Christian fellowship." (Never married, age thirty-six.)

"A real worship experience." (Divorced, age forty-two.)

"To accept life's situations as a stepping-stone to better things." (Widowed, age forty.)

"Social outlets and Bible teaching." (Never married, age forty-five.)

"A place to serve the Lord effectively as a single." (Divorced, age thirty-six.)

"A family. The people in my congregation are my family." (Never married, age thirty-nine.)

"Association with others in my position; peace of mind." (Divorced, age forty-nine.)

(Male respondents, ages thirty-five to fifty)

"Right relationship with God." (Never married, age forty-six.)

"Bible study." (Never married, age forty-four.)

"Inspiration and help in day-to-day living." (Never married, age forty-seven.)

"Single activities." (Widowed, age forty-one.)

"An attractive female with similar interests." (Divorced, age forty-two.)

(Female respondents, ages over fifty)

"A place to worship where the people aren't dogmatic." (Divorced, age fifty-one.)

"Learning to grow in Christ." (Divorced, age fifty-seven.)

"Christian fellowship and learning more about the Bible." (Widowed, age fifty-seven.)

"Spiritual renewal and acceptance." (Divorced, age sixty-one.)

"Encouragement, comfort, relationships, and entertainment." (Divorced, age fifty-two.)

"Love." (Widowed, age fifty-four.)

(Male respondents, ages over fifty).

"Christian fellowship." (Never married, age fifty-two.)

"Personal identity." (Separated, age fifty.)

"Emotional support to help in daily living." (Divorced, age fifty.)

2. What I would most like ministers and church leaders to understand about being single is . . .

(Female respondents, ages eighteen to thirty-five)

"The aloneness of being single, especially when divorced. People treat you like you've committed the unforgivable sin." (Divorced, age thirty-two.)

"Our needs are just as important as the family unit in the church." (Divorced, age thirty-one.)

"The need to feel an active part of the church." (Widowed, age twenty-two.)

"Don't peg young singles as 'college and career.'" (Never married, age twenty-four.)

"You can't assume that it's everyone's ideal to marry and have children." (Never married, age twenty-three.)

"Would like more all-church outlets for fellowship. Don't segregate us." (Never married, age thirty.)

"We are just as worthwhile and valuable as marrieds." (Never married, age thirty-two.)

"We're not married, but are very capable of handling responsibility and performing duties within the church structure." (Never married, age twenty-four.)

"We are well-adjusted, responsible adults." (Never married, age twenty-four.)

"It's hard to follow biblical teachings in dating relationships." (Never married, age twenty-six.)

"Single can be a gift, not a bad thing." (Never married, age twenty-four.)

"Singles have similar as well as different needs from married couples." (Never married, age twenty-four.)

"It's not a tragedy." (Never married, age twenty-seven.)

"We aren't outcasts." (Never married, age twenty-three.)

"It's not a crime." (Never married, age twenty-three.)

"That I'm not suddenly 'suspect' because I'm single." (Divorced, age thirty.)

"It's lonely after being married." (Divorced, age twenty-nine.)

"We are whole, not half persons." (Never married, age thirty-four.)

"We're not all 'playboys or playgirls.' " (Never married, age thirty.)

(Male respondents, ages eighteen to thirty-five)

"You must spend time getting to know us if you're trying to respond to us." (Never married, age twenty-seven.)

"We need to have opportunities to relate to the rest of the congregation." (Never married, age twenty-eight.)

"We're people just like marrieds are." (Never married, age twenty-seven.)

"That a single person can be stable and normal." (Never married, age twenty-seven.)

"I'm not strange." (Never married, age thirty-two.)

"Don't press marriage." (Never married, age twenty-nine.)

"Many activities are planned and scheduled only with couples in mind." (Never married, age twenty-seven.)

"The hurt of being alone." (Divorced, age thirty-five.)

(Female respondents, ages thirty-five to fifty)

"The church is structured for couples. You aren't aware of that when you're a couple. It hits you full force when you suddenly become single." (Divorced, age forty-two.)

"The difficulty of expressing sexuality and retaining Christian principles." (Never married, age thirty-six.)

"There is a feeling of not fitting into any program since they are all family oriented." (Widowed, age forty).

"That you can have male friends and not be doing anything immoral." (Divorced, age thirty-nine.)

"It's difficult to be single and Christian." (Divorced, age thirty-six.)

"It's difficult after twenty-one years of marriage to return to the single life." (Divorced, age forty-nine.)

"That we are human too." (Never married, age forty.)

"That we have something to contribute to the church just as married people do." (Divorced, age forty-nine.)

(Male respondents, ages thirty-five to fifty)

"I'm not attending church and Sunday School for the purpose of getting married." (Never married, age forty-six.)

"We are not an 'off-breed.'" (Never married, age forty-four.)

"That we are not different from others who need God's guidance." (Divorced, age forty-five.)

(Female respondents, ages over fifty)

"We're just like married people except that we may have had some heartaches that others haven't had to experience." (Divorced, age fifty-seven.)

"That we need extra training and leadership." (Divorced, age fifty-seven.)

"I need their prayers." (Widowed, age fifty-seven.)

"I may be older than thirty, but I'm still interested in life." (Divorced, age fifty-six.)

"This is not by choice." (Divorced, age sixty.)

"The older group needs consideration too." (Widowed, "young sixty.")

"I believe that they already understand." (Divorced, age fifty-two.)

(Male respondents, ages over fifty)
"It's extremely difficult." (Never married, age fifty-two.)

"That within their means, singles are better contributors in work and money than many marrieds." (Divorced, age seventy-one.)

"Jesus was a single adult." (Separated, age fifty.)

"Divorce is not always a frivolous solution; it's sometimes the only solution to improving one's life." (Divorced, age fifty.)

3. The main disadvantage or the most difficult part of being single is . . .

(Female respondents, ages eighteen to thirty-five)
"Being alone." (Divorced, age thirty-one.)

"Some think you're single because you're 'easy.' " (Never married, age twenty-four.)

"That everyone expects you to be married, either now or in the future." (Never married, age twenty-three.)

"People are more concerned about my marital status than with my growth as a Christian." (Never married, age twenty-eight.)

"Sex." (Divorced, age twenty-nine.)

"Loneliness." (Never married, age thirty-two.)

"Discrimination because people feel that single is what's left of the people who couldn't or wouldn't get married. Being accepted as a total person instead of just half of a pair." (Never married, age twenty-four.)

"Having to be totally self-sufficient." (Never married, age twenty-three.)

"Relatives expect you to be married." (Never married, age twenty-four.)

"No one to share the really good times or the really bad times with." (Never married, age twenty-five.)

"Being dateless." (Never married, age twenty-seven.)

"Activities geared toward couples." (Never married, age twenty-three.)

"Dealing with sex." (Divorced, age thirty-three.)

"Loneliness . . . feeling that something must be wrong with me." (Never married, age thirty-one.)

"I feel very selfish about doing things for myself." (Divorced, age twenty-nine.)

"Feeling at times like something must be wrong with me since I'm not married like everyone else." (Separated, age thirty-three.)

"The thought of eternal aloneness." (Never married, age twenty.)

"Playing games with people." (Divorced, age thirty-two.)

"Trying to explain to nonsingle people why you are single." (Never married, age twenty-three.)

"Making long-term decisions; feeling settled." (Never married, age twenty-two.)

(Male respondents, ages eighteen to thirty-five)

"Not feeling needed." (Never married, age twenty-seven.)

"Some people look down on singles like they are a sickness." (Never married, age twenty-three.)

"People think something is wrong with you." (Never married, age twenty-seven.)

"Loneliness." (Never married, age twenty-five.)

"The lack of a partner to share your innermost thoughts and feelings." (Never married, age twenty-seven.)

"I can't express myself sexually the way I'd like." (Never married, age twenty-one.)

"Getting routine household chores done." (Never married, age twenty-seven.)

"Sex." (Divorced, age thirty-five.)

"The stigma that we're weird or prone to abnormal sexual tendencies simply because we're not married." (Never married, age twenty-eight.)

"People acting like you're a freak since you're not married." (Never married, age twenty-nine.)

"Temptation to become sexually involved with a woman outside of marriage." (Never married, age twenty-four.)

"Cooking." (Never married, age twenty-three.)

(Female respondents, ages thirty-five to fifty)

"Total upbringing of the children." (Divorced, age forty-two.)

"Wanting to be with someone." (Never married, age thirty-six.)

"Accepting the fact." (Divorced, age forty-two.)

"Loneliness after twenty-eight years in a happy marriage." (Widowed, age forty-nine.)

"You can't talk to men without them thinking that you're interested in them." (Divorced, age thirty-nine.)

"Eating alone at home." (Divorced, age thirty-five.)

"Feeling unloved by one special person." (Divorced, age forty-nine.)

"Thinking about who will care for me when I get old, disabled, etc." (Never married, age forty-seven.)

(Male respondents, ages thirty-five to fifty)

"Living in a world which thinks by twos." (Never married, age forty.)

"Having to make all decisions." (Divorced, age forty-five.)

(Female respondents, ages over fifty)

"Sexual; it's impossible to live up to abstinence of sex." (Divorced, age fifty-one.)

"Just to have someone to talk to." (Divorced, age fifty-seven.)

"It's a world for married people." (Widowed, age fifty.)

"Sometimes feeling like an outsider." (Divorced, age fifty-seven.)

"Loneliness." (Widowed, age fifty.)

"No one to share good times with." (Divorced, age fifty-six.)

"Not being included as a vital part of the church." (Divorced, age sixty-one.)

"Too much responsibility." (Divorced, age fifty-two.)

"Decisions." (Widowed, age fifty-four.)

(Male respondents, ages over fifty)

"Loneliness and the need for a meaningful relationship." (Never married, age fifty-two.)

"Lack of companionship and love." (Divorced, age seventy-one.)

"Learning to function alone with decision making." (Divorced, age fifty.)

4. The biggest advantage of being single is . . .

(Female respondents, ages eighteen to thirty-five)

"Independence." (Divorced, age thirty-one.)

"Not tied down by family obligations." (Never married, age twenty-four.)

"I can completely control who I am and where I go." (Never married, age twenty-three.)

"Freedom to plan my own time." (Never married, age thirty.)

"Learning to be happy with yourself first so that being happy with others becomes easier." (Never married, age twenty-four.)

"Being alone, with time for myself, to get in touch with myself and to know I can live on my own." (Never married, age twenty-six.)

"Freedom and being responsible for only yourself." (Never married, age twenty-five.)

"Having the opportunity to develop your own talents and interests." (Never married, age twenty-five.)

"The freedom it allows you to grow as an individual, if a person will use it for that." (Never married, age twenty-five.)

"You're your own boss." (Never married, age twenty-seven.)

"You're only responsible for yourself." (Never married, age twenty-three.)

"Freedom to grow and make your own decisions." (Never married, age twenty-three.)

"The freedom to make changes (residence, job, etc.) easier." (Never married, age twenty-two.)

"Being able to make decisions freely without having to consult someone else." (Never married, age twenty-six.)

(Male respondents, ages eighteen to thirty-five)

"The time spent alone that helps so much in moving toward self-realization; freedom to do what I want when I want without any consultation." (Never married, age twenty-two.)

"Freedom." (Divorced, age thirty-five.)

"The ability to do about anything on a moment's notice." (Never married, age twenty-seven.)

"Cannot think of any." (Never married, age thirty-two.)

"I'm not responsible for anyone else—if I decide to look for a job in another town, I can just pick up and go without having to worry about someone else. I like my independence." (Never married, age twenty-one.)

"Privacy." (Never married, age twenty-five.)

"Mobility—location, social outings, career, etc." (Never married, age twenty-eight.)

"Freedom." (Never married, age thirty-four.)

(Female respondents, ages thirty-five to fifty)

"Being totally responsible for myself to make my own decisions, my own commitment, and also, of course, to face the consequences of all my actions." (Divorced, age forty-two.)

"?" (Divorced, age forty-two.)

"Doing what you want to when you want to. If I go home from work too tired to cook, I have no husband to have to wait on hand and foot like I did for many years. I know I'm alone with God now. So I take it from there." (Divorced, age thirty-nine.)

"None." (Widowed, age ?)

"To feel part of society and sometimes the church." (Widowed, age forty-one.)

"Being 'free' from some responsibilities to serve in other ways; being able to set the thermostat at the temperature *I* want; freedom to cook and sleep when I want to—or not to if I don't want to." (Divorced, age thirty-five.)

"Freedom to pursue own individual interests. (That may sound selfish.)" (Never married, forty-one.)

"A chance to find out who I am, to learn to like myself, and to realize my potential as a person." (Divorced, age thirty-six.)

"Developing as a real individual." (Divorced, age forty-nine.)

(Male respondents, ages thirty-five to fifty)

"Freedom to devote time to activities other than those geared around a home. Singles could be used much more advantageously in church—on committees, etc." (Never married, age forty-seven.)

"You aren't accountable for the mistakes of your family." (Never married, age forty-four.)

"Time does not have to be accounted for to someone else." (Divorced, age forty-five.)

"Freedom to choose your own life-style." (Divorced, age forty-one.)

(Female respondents, ages over fifty)

"You are always your own person." (Divorced, age fifty-one.)

"Independence." (Divorced, age seventy.)

"Not any." (Widowed, age fifty.)

"You have more time to actually work and learn more about being a Christian." (Divorced, age fifty-seven.)

"Time and money to work and serve more effectively."

(Never married, age sixty-five.)

"My time and money are not obligated to another person."
(Divorced, age fifty-six.)

"Can't think of any right now!" (Divorced, age sixty-one.)

"?" (Divorced, age fifty-three.)

"Can't think of any." (Widowed, "young" sixty-eight.)

"None, except one can attend the church of his own
choice—no one else's opinion or feelings to consider in making decisions." (Divorced, age fifty-two.)

(Male respondents, ages over fifty)

"Learning to find security; developing and finding confidence to enjoy life alone." (Divorced, age fifty.)

"None that I can see." (Never married, age fifty-two.)

"Freedom; choice of companion." (Divorced, age seventy-
one.)